The Academy Awards® Book of Lists: An Unauthorized, Unofficial, and Unprecedented History of the Oscars®

Part One

The Academy Awards® Book of Lists: An Unauthorized, Unofficial, and Unprecedented History of the Oscars®

Part One

by Chris Strodder

BearManor Media

2023

Library of Congress Registration

Name: Strodder, Chris (author)

Title: The Academy Awards® Book of Lists: An Unauthorized, Unofficial, and Unprecedented History of the Oscars®

Published in the United States of America by:

BearManor Media

4700 Millenia Blvd.
Suite 175 PMB 90497
Orlando, FL 32839

bearmanormedia.com

Printed in the United States.

Typesetting and layout by PKJ Passion Global

ISBN—979-8-88771-100-3

This book is intended to provide general information. The publisher, author, distributor, and copyright owner are not engaged in rendering professional advice or services. The publisher, author, distributor, and copyright owner are not liable or responsible to any person or group with respect to any loss, illness, or injury caused or alleged to be caused by the information found in this book.

The Academy Awards® Book of Lists is not endorsed by, authorized by, or associated with the Academy of Motion Picture Arts and Sciences (A.M.P.A.S.). The Oscar statuette and the terms Oscar®, Oscars®, and Academy Awards® are registered trademarks and service marks of A.M.P.A.S. Their use in this book is a nominative fair use of said marks. No authorization is required or was obtained from the owners of said marks.

Similarly, this book makes reference to many copyrighted movie characters, movie titles, book titles, and more that are the property of their respective owners. Any previously copyrighted or trademarked material mentioned or shown in this book is used solely for editorial and informational purposes under the Fair Use Doctrine. Neither the author nor the publisher makes any commercial claim to their use. See the Photo List page for information about the photographs and images used in the book.

TABLE OF CONTENTS: A LIST OF THE LISTS

PART ONE

INTRODUCTION: TWO LISTS ABOUT THIS LIST BOOK

OSCAR CATEGORIES, ELIGIBILITY, AND VOTING

OSCAR-WINNING AND OSCAR-NOMINATED MOVIES IN GENERAL

BEST ACTOR, ACTRESS, SUPPORTING ACTOR, AND SUPPORTING ACTRESS

BEST WRITING

PART TWO

CRAFTS, PART ONE: CINEMATOGRAPHY AND FILM EDITING

CRAFTS, PART TWO: PRODUCTION DESIGN, COSTUMES, AND MAKEUP

CRAFTS, PART THREE: VISUAL EFFECTS AND SOUND

CRAFTS, PART FOUR: MUSIC

BIBLIOGRAPHY

PHOTO LIST

INDEX

ABOUT THE AUTHOR

INTRODUCTION: TWO LISTS ABOUT THIS LIST BOOK

Aaannnddd ACTION! 11 Introductory Notes from the Author

1. The Academy Awards offer a mother lode of glittering history that writers have been mining for almost a century to produce countless articles, essays, pre-ceremony predictions, post-ceremony analyses, trivia quizzes, pictorial fashion books, and year-by-year recaps. The sheer volume and variety of published material about the Oscars would suggest that every nugget of information has already been uncovered and reported about the world's most famous award and its widely seen, closely scrutinized, profusely discussed ceremony. Surely that rich Oscar vein has been played out by now, right?

2. Welcome to *The Academy Awards® Book of Lists*, a different way to study and celebrate the Oscars. Here's one quick example of how this book of creative lists is distinctive: traditional Oscar histories typically scatter the awkward moments that have occurred at various Academy Awards ceremonies across hundreds of chronological pages, but Part Two of the book you're holding gathers those gems into one convenient list on page 560 that's literally called "25 Awkward Moments at the Academy Awards Ceremony." *Voilà.*

3. While the book is new, my idea for it isn't. I've been working towards something like *The Academy Awards® Book of Lists* ever since I watched my first televised Oscar ceremony as a child in 1965. That year *My Fair Lady* (1964) was named Best Picture over

my own pick, a totally awesome movie my family had seen in a theater. Sadly, *The Incredible Mr. Limpet* wasn't up for anything.

As I struggled to make sense of the dazzling, sometimes bewildering ceremony on TV, I created a rudimentary list of other 1964 movies I'd seen. For the next year's telecast, I made a new list for 1965 movies and subdivided it into several sections that compared the Oscar-winning movies in simple ways (which ones had the longest titles, were about real people, were comedies, etc.), with everything handwritten on lined binder paper and kept in its own special Pee-Chee folder. Year by year that folder steadily expanded as I scrutinized every Oscar broadcast, read everything I could find about the awards and the ceremonies, and supplemented my ever-developing, ever-amendable lists.

4. In the '80s my Oscar attention ratcheted from interest to passion when I started interning for Hollywood's *Movieline* magazine, a providential break that frequently sent me to the Margaret Herrick Research Library inside the Academy of Motion Pictures Arts and Sciences headquarters on Wilshire Boulevard. *Movieline* also brought me my first studio visits, preview screenings, celebrity interviews, and published bylines.

    Jump-cut ahead almost four decades, past eight other nonfiction books I wrote on various pop culture topics (including movies), and there I was in 2021, a lifelong film fanatic, an attentive viewer of fifty-six consecutive Academy Awards ceremonies, a charter member of the Academy Museum of Motion Pictures, but still just a kid with a crazy dream of fashioning my comprehensive Oscar lists into a unique history book.

5. *The Academy Awards® Book of Lists* is not a collection of personal "top tens" that rank movies in various categories. First off, the lists aren't my own subjective selections; the lists illuminate Oscar history, not Oscar opinions.

    What's more, the Oscar lists in these two books aren't confined to ten items. They are, however, confined to the awards and the ceremonies; there are no gossipy lists that ridicule red-carpet fashions or scandalize the stars' private lives, because it's just not that kind of book.

6. Most of the lists are grouped by Oscar category (Best Director, Best Cinematography, Best Animated Feature Film, etc.), and there are three main types of lists: lists of interesting facts (for example, "13 Actresses Who Won Oscars for Their First Performance"); lists of informed observations ("100 Memorable Movies That Didn't Get Nominated for Best Picture"); and lists written by actual Oscar winners who kindly responded to my written requests to contribute a list for the book. I asked, they listed, readers benefited.

7. Because simple inventories of past Oscar winners and nominees are easy to find on the Internet, I invented many original topics in hopes of pushing beyond the familiar towards the unusual. To get a glimpse of what I'm talking about, skip ahead to page 589 in the Moviellaneous section for a list called "20 Examples of 'The Oscars of' Something Besides Movies," which lists actual awards that are called "the Oscars" of their fields ("the Oscars of Infectious Diseases," really?).

8. Short intros preface the lists to give them some context and connect the historical dots. Other books on various topics rou-

tinely compile lists, but they don't always provide insightful explanations.

For example, Dave Marsh and Kevin Stein's *The Book of Rock Lists*, a wide-ranging, endlessly entertaining volume published by *Rolling Stone* magazine in 1981, ranks Elvis's *King Creole* (1958) first and the Beatles' Oscar-nominated *A Hard Day's Night* (1964) fourth on its "Best Rock and Roll Movies" list without justifying either position. A little reasoning would have made those rankings easier to accept. Thus *The Academy Awards® Book of Lists* includes the *why* was as well as the *what* wherever possible. Ideally the movie novice will be as enlightened as the expert will be convinced.

9. Having written articles, nonfiction books, short stories, children's books, and novels, I have found the list book to be its own fascinating and rewarding genre. I first experienced the joy of detailed listmaking when I wrote *The Disneyland Book of Lists* in 2015, and I still happily continue to make lists on all sorts of subjects. I highly recommend it.

Actually, you might already be listing—ever written down the detailed goals you want to achieve or the precise places you'd like to visit? Thoughtfully prioritized on paper the things you have to do during the day? Carefully organized songs by theme, by artist, by mood? What you've got there are lists, my friend, making you a "lister."

10. James Joyce called errors "the portals of discovery." I think of them the same way. Should you doubt a fact or notice a possible "portal of discovery," please do two things: first, forgive my mistake (and it is my mistake, nobody else's); and second, let me know what you found by politely writing to me via theacademyawardsbookoflists@gmail.com. I'll reply with interest and gratitude.

11. *The Oxford English Dictionary* defines archaic forms of the word "list" and says it was first used to mean "cataloguing" in the

1500s. Other usages include a variation of "lust"; a strip of cloth; a boundary; and "listy," which in the *OED* means "pleasant" or "delightful." Hopefully you'll find these two list books listy.

—C.S., April 2023

6 Historical Lists

Before we jump into the bulk of the text, a quick pause to refamiliarize you with the concept of listmaking. The practice of ordering things into lists—"listing"—has a long history. With many to choose from, we present a half-dozen chronologically ordered examples ranging from the sublime to the ridiculous, all of them created long before dim moving images on short reels of crude film first began to flicker past Thomas Edison's eyes in 1889. That pre-twentieth century cutoff eliminates such famous lists as the one in the 1934 song "Santa Claus Is Coming to Town" ("he's making a list, he's checking it twice") and the 1971 "enemies list" created by Richard Nixon.

1. **Ten Commandments**
- From the Old Testament's *Book of Exodus*, circa 600-500 B.C.
2. **Seven Wonders of the Ancient World**
- Described circa 200-100 B.C.
3. **Seven Deadly Sins**
- Defined by Pope Gregory I, 590 A.D.
4. **"Fifty-Seven Sins of Isaac Newton, as Recorded by Himself"**
- From "Stealing cherry cobs" and "Punching my sister" to "Falling out with the servants" and "Twisting a cord on Sunday," compiled by the twenty-year-old Newton in a notebook called *The Fitzwilliam Manuscript*, circa 1662.
5. **Thirteen "Necessary or Desirable" Virtues of Benjamin Franklin**
- Starting with Temperance and ending with Humility, published in *The Autobiography of Benjamin Franklin*, 1793.

6. **Thirteen "Chief Circumstances Connected with Spontaneous Combustion"**

- According to a scientific study published by Dr. Robert Macnish in 1834, number two on his list claims that far more women than men spontaneously combust, and number eight cautions that "spontaneous combustions are more frequent in winter than in summer."

And now, without further ado, we follow the commands given by the Ghost thirty-five minutes into the Best Picture-winning *Hamlet* (1948): "List, list, oh, list!"

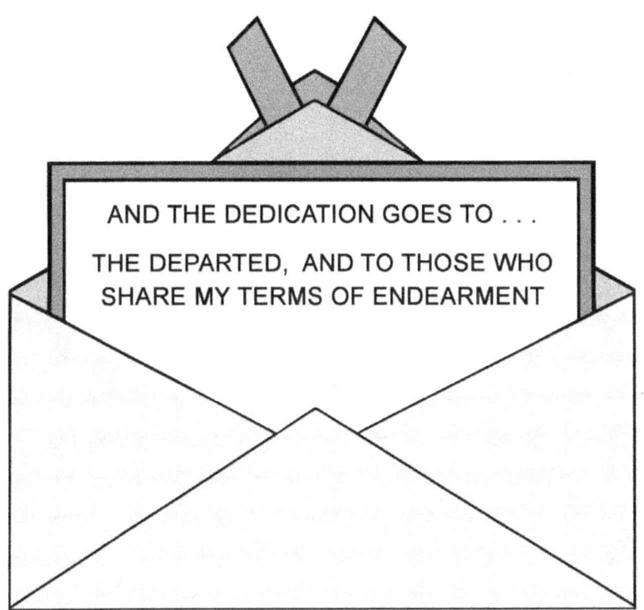

AND THE DEDICATION GOES TO . . .
THE DEPARTED, AND TO THOSE WHO
SHARE MY TERMS OF ENDEARMENT

OSCAR CATEGORIES, ELIGIBILITY, AND VOTING

Disquiet on the Western Front: 6 Factors and Features as the Academy Was Being Formed

Throughout these two books we make hundreds of references to "the Academy." This Academy of which we speak, and the one that most Oscar recipients thank in their acceptance speeches, is the Academy of Motion Picture Arts and Sciences.

Volumes could be written about the Academy's long history, its many publications, its vast library and impressive education programs, its wide-ranging charity work, its distinctive museum, and more. But we've chosen to focus on its most famous symbol, the Oscar. To that end, we present a brief summary of factors and features of the Academy's formation in 1927, which soon led to the creation of its coveted award in 1928 and its first awards presentation in 1929.

1. Movie popularity

Loved by many, seen by almost everybody, and snubbed apathetically by virtually nobody, movies (all of them silent, and either in black and white or very limited color) were thriving in the mid-1920s.

- In 1926 movie attendance soared past fifty million tickets sold per week, this at a time when the entire U.S. population was about 117 million.

- Stars weren't just admired, they were revered, and their movies weren't just popular, they were essential: Hollywood's long-reigning queen, Mary Pickford, was in such unbelievable demand that she made, on average, one short film or feature-length movie per month every single year from 1909 to 1929, including fifty-one silents just in 1911 alone.
- By 1926 tests were already being made for the exciting new "talkies" that would debut a year later and bring with them new technology, new professions, and revamped studios and theaters.
- Talking pictures would also generate an explosive surge in movie attendance; by decade's end, with opulent new movie palaces being built all across the country, weekly attendance would hit a hundred million, or about 80 percent of the population.

2. Jazz Age reformers

While movies were helping to energize the "Roaring Twenties," cultural reform was a big topic in the decade's early years.

- In 1920, women finally gained the vote, and America lost alcohol as Prohibition began.
- In 1921, major league baseball hoped to restore its scandalized sport by handing down harsh penalties to the cheating "Black Sox" players who had tried to "fix" the 1919 World Series.
- In 1922, a stern former cabinet member named Will Hays was appointed as the first president of the Motion Picture Producers and Distributors of America, a new association created by the heads of the major movie studios. As Hollywood's official watchdog, Hays was given the mandate to oversee the troubled movie industry and enforce "the highest possible moral and aesthetic standards in motion picture production."

3. The years of living dangerously

Hays' appointment was a response to a nation-wide call from religious, women's, and parents' groups to "clean up" Hollywood, a town whose main industry, despite all the gallant heroes, glamorous heroines, and romantic stories celebrated on film, was coming to symbolize sinful decadence. Movies throughout the early 1920s were becoming increasingly earthy, risqué, even erotic as they devoted more and more screen time to scenes of scantily clad actresses

The Sheik (1921).

and unrestrained debauchery. In addition, notorious real-life scandals were ruining carefully framed reel-life reputations. Dozens of gossipy movie magazines described the lavish, hedonistic lives of dissolute, free-spending movie stars, and tabloid newspapers were recounting in lurid detail private and public celebrity excesses. Among the decade's headline-grabbers . . .

- 1920: the death of silent film star Olive Thomas, ruled as accidental but sensationalized in the press as a possible suicide or drug overdose.
- 1921: the widely publicized affair between silent film star Blanche Sweet and director Marshall Neilan, who was already

married to (and soon to be divorced from) actress Gertrude Bambrick.

- 1921/1922: the three extensively covered Roscoe "Fatty" Arbuckle trials after the death of actress Virginia Rappe at a wild party.
- 1922: the unsolved murder of director William Desmond Taylor in his Hollywood home.
- 1922: the arrest of movie heartthrob Rudolph Valentino, star of *The Sheik* (1921), on bigamy charges.
- 1923: the drug-related demise of handsome silent film star Wallace Reid.
- 1924: the suspicious death of producer Thomas Ince aboard William Randolph Hearst's yacht.
- 1925: the tragic collapse and death of fourteen-year-old child star Lucille Ricksen, who may have died of extreme exhaustion from overwork (rumors suggested more alarming causes).
- 1926: the sudden death (quickly assumed to be from a drug overdose) of beautiful, fast-living movie star Barbara LaMarr.

Waging his war on multiple fronts, Hays tried to rein in out-of-control stars by adding strict morality clauses to contracts that would punish bad behavior, and he started advising studios about what they shouldn't be showing in their movies. To nudge studios away from taboo subjects, in 1927 he pushed thirty-six recommendations called "Don'ts and Be Carefuls"; three years later he clamped down with his even harsher Production Code (aka the Hays Code), which effectively sanitized movies for decades with a long list of specific things that could not be shown and said on film.

4. Initial discussions

Even as Will Hays was already exercising his restrictive powers, in the mid-1920s nervous Hollywood leaders, especially Metro-Gold-wyn-Mayer (MGM) titan Louis B. Mayer, feared that further negative publicity and the resulting public backlash might generate costly boycotts or strong government interventions, possibly even intrusive censorship. According to "You Must Remember This" podcaster Karina Longworth, writing at Slate.com, "The more the media harped on the Fatty Arbuckle rape allegations or Wallace Reid's heroin problem, the more Mayer was convinced that angry Christian mobs would eventually rise up and burn Hollywood to the ground. 'If this keeps up, there won't be any more film business,' he said."

- Not only did Mayer and other important players sense that a train wreck was coming, they realized that they themselves were driving the train and needed to slow it down before their business was permanently derailed. The powerful Mayer pushed for a unifying organization that would promote a positive image for Hollywood and generate good will with the community via donations and benefits. Ideally this organization would even be, according to Mayer, a "convenient mediator and harmonizer" to resolve labor disputes between actors, directors, writers, craftspeople, and the studios. And theoretically it would help foster the industry-wide cooperation needed to ease the difficult and expensive transition from silent to sound films.
- Louis B. Mayer and three others met informally in early January, 1927 to discuss the creation of this still-unnamed organization.

5. Formal meetings

On January 11, 1927, this four-man group held a more formal meeting at the Ambassador Hotel with thirty-two other key Hollywood players.

- Among them were twenty-six-year-old "boy wonder" Irving Thalberg (for whom the Thalberg Award would later be named); respected directors Cecil B. DeMille and Raoul Walsh; beloved movie stars Douglas Fairbanks, Harold Lloyd, and Mary Pickford; theater impresario Sid Grauman; and various prominent writers, technicians, and lawyers.
- The group unanimously agreed on the need for a new organization and continued to meet throughout the spring. By mid-May they had decided on the dignified name Academy of Motion Picture Arts and Sciences, officially registered as a non-profit corporation, and elected Fairbanks as the Academy's first president.

6. Awards of Merit

By the summer of 1927 the Academy had rented small offices on Hollywood Boulevard less than a mile from the intersection of Hollywood Boulevard and Vine Street. Before the year was out the expanding Academy had moved to a floor of the Roosevelt Hotel across the street from the newly opened Grauman's Chinese Theater.

- In 1927 the Academy's dues-paying membership ($100 annually) numbered in the hundreds.
- That same year the Academy decided that one way to improve Hollywood's image was to celebrate "distinctive achievement" with Awards of Merit. Not only would these new awards inspire filmmakers and encourage their artistic instincts, they would educate the public about the industry's best and noblest movies.
- In the summer of 1928, the awards committee, originally headed by MGM art director (and future Oscar designer and winner) Cedric Gibbons, finally settled on twelve awards categories and basic guidelines for eligibility and voting (all discussed in upcoming lists), with the first awards to be presented the following year.

6 Key Differences Between the First and the Ninety-Second Oscar Ceremonies

To get oriented to the Academy's procedures and presentations, this list offers some historical perspective by contrasting the first and ninety-second Oscar ceremonies. The ninety-second ceremony serves as an appropriate ending point because that was the last "traditional" pre-COVID ceremony before dramatic changes were made the following year. See the list called "6 Major Changes Specific to the Ninety-Third Oscar Ceremony" on page 541 for more on 2021's unique event.

1. Eligibility dates for nominated movies

First ceremony: movies released in the twelve months from August 1, 1927 to July 31, 1928

- The 1929 ceremony followed about thirty-eight weeks (almost ten months) after the end of the eligibility period.

Ninety-second ceremony: the twelve months from January 1, 2019-December 31, 2019

- The 2020 ceremony followed about five weeks (just over one month) after the end of the eligibility period.

2. Nominations announcement

First: February 18, 1929, eighty-seven days (about three months) before the ceremony

- Not just the nominees but also the *winners* were announced in advance, meaning there were no surprises when the awards were actually handed out.

Ninety-second: January 13, 2020, twenty-seven days (about one month) before the awards ceremony

- A televised early-morning ceremony presented the names of the nominees; other than those tabulating the final votes, nobody knew who the winners would be until they were announced at the ceremony.

3. Number of awards categories

First: twelve, representing twenty-five different nominated movies, all of them in black and white, and all of them silent except for *The Jazz Singer* (1927). The twelve categories at the first ceremony:

- Outstanding Picture
- Unique and Artistic Picture
- Best Actor
- Best Actress
- Best Director (Comedy Picture)
- Best Director (Dramatic Picture)
- Best Writing (Original Story)
- Best Writing (Adaptation)
- Best Art Direction
- Best Cinematography
- Best Engineering Effects
- Best Title Writing

Ninety-second: twenty-four, representing fifty-three different nominated movies (including documentaries, animated movies, and short films). The two-dozen categories at the ninety-second ceremony:

- Best Picture
- Best Actor

- Best Actress
- Best Supporting Actor
- Best Supporting Actress
- Best Director
- Best Writing (Adapted Screenplay)
- Best Writing (Original Screenplay)
- Best Film Editing
- Best Cinematography
- Best Production Design
- Best Makeup and Hairstyling
- Best Costume Design
- Best Visual Effects
- Best Documentary (Feature)
- Best Documentary (Short Subject)
- Best Short Film (Live Action)
- Best Short Film (Animated)
- Best Original Score
- Best Original Song
- Best Sound Editing
- Best Sound Mixing
- Best Animated Feature Film
- Best International Feature Film

4. Ceremony date

First: Thursday, May 16, 1929

- A festive banquet with dinner and dancing at the Hollywood Roosevelt Hotel, more of a party than an awards presentation; hosted by Academy President Douglas Fairbanks, assisted by director William C. de Mille.

Ninety-second: Sunday, February 9, 2020

- A formal presentation at the Dolby Theatre in Hollywood; no dinner, no dancing, no host.
- Historically, this February date was the earliest the ceremony had ever been held (the latest date was November 18, 1932).

5. Audience

First: 270 guests

- Many attendees had paid $5 for a ticket; no live radio or TV coverage.

Ninety-second: approximately 3,400 guests

- All guests were invited, so nobody paid for a ticket; a global audience watched on TV.

6. Amount of time needed to present all the awards

First: under fifteen minutes (some estimates say it took only *five* minutes)

- After the dinner and dancing, the event's host, Douglas Fairbanks, handed out all the Awards of Merit and the Special Awards one after another in a brisk no-fuss ceremony. Only one winner—producer Darryl F. Zanuck, receiving a Special Award on behalf of Warner Bros. and *The Jazz Singer* (1927)—gave a short acceptance speech. A few more praising comments by industry insiders followed the brief awards presentation, and the evening wrapped up with a song by Al Jolson.

Ninety-second: 212 minutes

- No dinner or dancing, just the three-and-a-half hour ceremony that included a comedic opening, thirty awards presenters, performances of all five nominated songs, acceptance speeches by the winners, an "In Memorium" tribute, and more.

7 Major Changes to the Academy's Early Voting Procedure

In its first three decades of Oscar ceremonies, the Academy continually tweaked the voting procedure that selected the nominees and winners (it even tweaked the name—originally the awards were called Academy Awards of Merit, what the Academy stated "should be considered the highest distinction attainable in the motion picture profession"). Below are seven major changes in the way Oscar nominees and winners were chosen in those early years.

1. First ceremony (held in 1929)

The entire Academy membership (originally 230 people) recommended movies for awards.

- Twenty judges (appointed by the Academy) narrowed the list to the official nominees.
- Five men who represented the Academy's five branches (Actors, Directors, Producers, Technicians, and Writers) then selected the winners from the list of official nominees.

2. Third ceremony (held in 1930)

The previous voting process (twenty nominating judges and a five-man final-voting committee) was abandoned.

- All Academy members (over four hundred people) chose nominees and winners.

3. Seventh ceremony (held in 1935)

For the seventh and eighth ceremonies, voters were told they could ignore the official nominees if they wanted and instead could write in any winners from any movies.

- Despite the opportunities for write-ins during this two-year period, there was only one write-in winner: Hal Mohr, Best Cinematography, *A Midsummer Night's Dream* (1935).
- All other winners came from the list of official nominees.

4. Ninth ceremony (held in 1937)

A new committee of fifty Academy members (drawn from the Academy's five branches) selected nominees.

- All members then voted on the winners.

5. Tenth ceremony (held in 1938)

About ten thousand non-members of the Academy were allowed to join with the existing members to choose nominees and winners.

- These non-members, representing various unions and guilds from the movie-making industry, swelled the number of voters to well over 11,000 people.

6. Nineteenth ceremony (held in 1947)

The non-Academy members added to the voting procedure in 1938 still helped choose the nominees.

- The final votes on the winners were cast by the approximately 1,600 Academy members.

7. Thirtieth ceremony (held in 1958)

Non-Academy members were eliminated from the voting process.

- Academy members (at the time about 1,800 people) chose all nominees and winners.
- This is the current voting procedure, with additional complications that the next list attempts to simplify.

6 Major Components of the Current Voting Procedure

What seems like a straightforward two-step procedure—Academy members vote on eligible movies to select nominees, and then vote on nominees to select winners—is actually an extremely complicated process. Without delving into the abstruse "preferential voting system" that asks voters to rank the nominees, not merely choose a single favorite, we present a simplified summary of the current voting procedure that's used to select recipients of Academy Awards.

1. Current Academy membership

About 10,500 people

- Nearly all of them are active professionals working in the movie industry.

- About a thousand members have "emeritus" or "associate" status and so don't vote, leaving about 9,500 current Academy members whose votes decide the winners.

2. New members

Nomination and approval

- New members join after they're nominated and approved by an executive committee composed of current members.
- Oscar nominees automatically become members eligible to vote.

3. Branches

Members are divided into eighteen branches.

- Fourteen branches are represented at the ceremony with one or more awards categories: actors (the largest branch, with over 1,300 active members), cinematographers, costume designers, directors, documentarians, editors, makeup artists/hairstylists, composers/songwriters, producers (the Best Picture award), production designers, makers of short films and feature animation, sound editors/sound designers, visual effects artists, and writers.
- Four additional branches are not represented at the ceremony with any award categories: casting directors; marketing/public relations specialists; studio executives; and, as of March 2023, a new production and technology branch that includes associate producers, choreographers, colorists, music supervisors, script supervisors, and stunt coordinators.
- Even if one person could belong to two or more branches—someone like the multitalented artist shown on the next page, Roberto Benigni, whose *Life Is Beautiful* (1997) brought him a Best Actor win and Best Director and Best Writing nominations—nobody can belong to more than one branch.

Roberto Benigni in Roberto Benigni's LIFE IS BEAUTIFUL (LA VITA È BELLA).

4. Choosing nominees

Branches nominate branches

- Academy members in the various branches choose nominees for their particular branch (directors nominate candidates for Best Director, and cinematographers nominate candidates for Best Cinematography, for example).
- The idea is that experts in the specific fields will select the worthiest nominees.
- The one exception is Best Picture—all Academy members nominate movies for this important award.

5. Exceptions

Special committees and shortlists
- The categories for animated films, documentaries, international feature films, and short films have a slightly different process that involves nominations generated by special committees.

- In addition, the Academy announces a "shortlist" of movies under consideration in some categories; this pool of movies (usually ten to fifteen) is then narrowed down to the final nominees.
- A month before the ninety-fourth ceremony (held in 2022), these ten categories had shortlists: Documentary (Feature); Documentary (Short Subject); International Feature Film; Makeup and Hairstyling; Music (Original Score); Music (Original Song); Short Film (Animated); Short Film (Live Action); Sound; and Visual Effects.

6. Choosing winners

Nominees are announced in January or February. Final voting on the winners ends within days of the ceremony (in 2023 the voting deadline was March 5th for the March 12th ceremony).

- The entire voting membership can cast final ballots in virtually all categories, including Best Picture.
- Since the eighty-fifth ceremony (held in 2013), members have been able to cast their votes either with traditional paper ballots or online.
- Voting results are essentially secret, known only to two representatives from the accounting firm of PricewaterhouseCoopers until they're announced at the ceremony.

7 Major Changes to the Academy's Eligibility Dates

Fans of the Oscars telecast are used to seeing nominees and winners drawn from movies that were released in the previous calendar year. But the Academy's eligibility period wasn't always so simple. The earliest Oscar ceremonies went back almost *two* years for their eligible movies. What's more, the third ceremony (held in 1930) included eligible movies that had been released *in the same year* as the ceremony itself, an attempt to bring the November ceremony closer to the end of the eligibility period for the movies being considered (the eligibility period ended in July). As shown below, the ninety-third ceremony (held in 2021) also had an eligibility period and a ceremony in the same year, but for a different reason.

In the following list, note how the eligibility dates and the ceremony dates move in relation to each other: at the first ceremony, there was a gap of almost ten months between the last eligibility date and the awards ceremony, but at the ninety-third ceremony that gap was less than two months. It's also interesting to see how the months of the ceremony have changed from spring to fall to spring to late winter and back to spring (see the list called "5 Months of the Year, and 7 Days of the Week, for the Oscar Ceremony" on page 534 for more on these shifting seasons).

1. First ceremony (May 16, 1929)

Eligibility period: twelve months
- August 1, 1927 to July 31, 1928
- Days from the end of the eligibility period to the next ceremony: 289

2. Second ceremony (April 3, 1930)

Eligibility period: twelve months
- August 1, 1928 to July 31, 1929
- Days from the end of the eligibility period to the next ceremony: 246

3. Third ceremony (November 5, 1930)

Eligibility period: twelve months
- August 1, 1929 to July 31, 1930
- Days from the end of the eligibility period to the next ceremony: 97

- This pattern of eligible movies and ceremonies all in the same year continued until the sixth ceremony.
- Note that there were two ceremonies, the second and the third, held in 1930 just seven months apart. No other year has had two ceremonies.

4. Sixth ceremony (March 16, 1934)

Eligibility period: seventeen months
- August 1, 1932 to December 31, 1933
- Days from the end of the eligibility period to the next ceremony: 75
- The seventeen-month eligibility period was a one-time change from the usual twelve-month eligibility period as the Academy prepared to switch to an eligibility period of a single calendar year, which went into effect at the next ceremony.
- If you count the ceremonies from the third one (held in late 1930), then the fourth was correctly held in 1931, the fifth was in 1932, and the sixth would have been in 1933. Notice, however, that the sixth ceremony was held in 1934, because the Academy skipped a 1933 ceremony so that it could rearrange its eligibility period to a January-to-December calendar year, with ceremonies to be held from February to April instead of in November.

5. Seventh ceremony (February 27, 1935) to the ninety-second ceremony (February 9, 2020)

Eligibility period: twelve months
- January 1 to December 31 of the previous calendar year
- Days from the end of the eligibility period to the next ceremony: varying, but usually in the forties-fifties for February ceremonies, sixties-eighties for March ceremonies, and nineties-low hundreds for April ceremonies.

6. Ninety-third ceremony (April 25, 2021)

Eligibility period: fourteen months
- January 1, 2020 to February 28, 2021
- Days from the end of the eligibility period to the next ceremony: 56
- This one-time change to a fourteen-month eligibility period was made to accommodate problems with theatrical releases due to the COVID-19 pandemic.

7. Ninety-fourth ceremony (March 27, 2022)

Eligibility period: ten months
- March 1, 2021 to December 31, 2021
- Days from the end of the eligibility period to the next ceremony: 86
- Subsequent ceremonies returned to the usual one-year January-December eligibility period.

21 Oscar Categories Added to the Original Twelve

As mentioned midway through the earlier list called "6 Key Differences Between the First and the Ninety-Second Oscar Ceremonies," the Academy's initial competitive categories numbered only twelve. Over the years, twenty-one additional Oscar categories joined the original dozen, and they're listed below according to the year each one was added. The ceremonies noted are the *first* ceremonies to include the new categories, and the movie titles are the first winners of these new awards.

Not all of these new categories were permanent, of course; some soon disappeared entirely (Best Assistant Director, for example), and some new categories were later renamed (Best Makeup expanded to Best Makeup and Hairstyling). The ceremony with the most categories, by the way, was the twenty-ninth (held in 1957), when the Academy awarded twenty-seven competitive Oscars.

1. Sound Recording

Third ceremony (held in 1930)
- *The Big House* (1930)

2. Short Subject (Cartoon)

Fifth ceremony (held in 1932)
- *Flowers and Trees* (1932)

3. Assistant Director

Sixth ceremony (held in 1934)
- Co-winners Charles Barton, Scott Beal, Charles Dorian, Fred Fox, Gordon Hollingshead, Dewey Starkey, and William Tummel (no specific movies identified)

4. Film Editing

Seventh ceremony (held in 1935)
- *Eskimo* (1933)

5. Music (Original Song)

Seventh ceremony (held in 1935)
- *The Gay Divorcee* (1934)

6. Music (Scoring)

Seventh ceremony (held in 1935)

- *One Night of Love* (1934)

7. Dance Direction

Eighth ceremony (held in 1936)
- *Broadway Melody of 1936* (1935)

8. Supporting Actor

Ninth ceremony (held in 1937)
- *Come and Get It* (1936)

9. Supporting Actress

Ninth ceremony (held in 1937)
- *Anthony Adverse* (1936)

10. Music (Original Score)

Eleventh ceremony (held in 1939)
- *The Adventures of Robin Hood* (1938)

11. Special Effects

Twelfth ceremony (held in 1940)
- *The Rains Came* (1939)

12. Documentary

Fourteenth ceremony (held in 1942)
- *Churchill's Island* (1941)

13. Costume Design

Twenty-first ceremony (held in 1949)
- *Hamlet* (1948)

14. Foreign Language Film

Twenty-ninth ceremony (held in 1957)
- *La Strada* (1954)

15. Short Subject (Live Action)

Thirtieth ceremony (held in 1958)
- *The Wetback Hound* (1957)

Hamlet (1948).

16. Sound Effects

Thirty-sixth ceremony (held in 1964)
- *It's a Mad, Mad, Mad, Mad World* (1963)

17. Makeup

Fifty-fourth ceremony (held in 1982)
- *An American Werewolf in London* (1981)

18. Sound Effects Editing

Fifty-fifth ceremony (held in 1983)
- *E.T. the Extra-Terrestrial* (1982)

19. Original Musical

Seventy-third ceremony (held in 2001)
- The Academy established this little-known category with the stipulation that during the year there must be at least ten movie musicals, and they must be originals, like *La La Land* (2016), not adaptations, like *Chicago* (2002). Because there hasn't been a single year with ten potential nominees, so far this Oscar has never been awarded. Think of that: an Oscar up for grabs, and nobody's been able to claim it once in over two decades.

20. Animated Feature Film

Seventy-fourth ceremony (held in 2002)
- *Shrek* (2001)

21. Sound Mixing

Seventy-sixth ceremony (held in 2004)
- *The Lord of the Rings: The Return of the King* (2003)

7 Early Oscar Categories That Soon Became Extinct

While the previous list shows twenty-one additions to the roster of competitive Oscar categories, this next list shows seven subtractions. These were all categories used in the first ten years of the Academy Awards, but all soon became extinct. Below each category is the number of ceremonies it was actually part of and the last winner in each category.

1. Director, Comedy Picture

One ceremony, the first (held in 1929)
- Lewis Milestone, *Two Arabian Knights* (1927)

2. Director, Dramatic Picture

One ceremony, the first (held in 1929)
- Frank Borzage, *7th Heaven* (1927)
- After the first ceremony, Best Director (Comedy Picture) and Best Director (Dramatic Picture) were united into a single Best Director category.

3. Engineering Effects (honoring visual effects)

One ceremony, the first (held in 1929)
- Roy Pomeroy, *Wings* (1927)

4. Title Writing (honoring the interstitial text cards shown in silent movies)

One ceremony, the first (held in 1929)
- Joseph Farnham (no specific movie identified)

5. Unique and Artistic Picture

One ceremony, the first (held in 1929)
- *Sunrise* (1927)

6. Assistant Director

Five ceremonies, the sixth to the tenth (held from 1934 to 1938)
- Robert D. Webb, *In Old Chicago* (1938)

7. Dance Direction

Three ceremonies, the eighth to the tenth (held from 1936 to 1938)
- Hermes Pan, *A Damsel in Distress* (1937)

Sunrise (1927).

OSCAR-WINNING AND OSCAR-NOMINATED MOVIES IN GENERAL

9 Oscar-Winning Movies with the Shortest Titles

Feature-length movies (including documentaries) with short titles and long legacies as Oscar winners. The following nine movies have but one, two, or three characters in their titles. If only the great *M* (1931) had been nominated and won something, then the list would total an even ten.

Just missing the cut at four characters are the three Best Picture winners with the shortest titles: *Gigi* (1958); *Argo* (2012); and *CODA* (2021). See the Appendix for the specific Oscars won by the following movies.

ONE CHARACTER

1. *Z* (1969)

TWO CHARACTERS

2. *Up* (2009)

THREE CHARACTERS

3. *Amy* (2015)
4. *Her* (2013)
5. *Hud* (1963)

6. *Ida* (2013)
7. *JFK* (1991)
8. *Ran* (1985)
9. *Ray* (2004)

4 Oscar-Winning Movies with the Longest Titles

Though we're gathering these next four movies together on the basis of their long titles, don't underestimate their overall excellence: all of them won Oscars in various categories (see the Appendix to find out which ones), and number two has to be the best movie ever made about a bus named Priscilla. Documentaries aren't included among these feature-length movies, otherwise this list would have been three times as long.

FIFTY-TWO CHARACTERS

1. *The Chronicles of Narnia: The Lion, the Witch and the Wardrobe* (2005)

FORTY-ONE CHARACTERS

2. *The Adventures of Priscilla, Queen of the Desert* (1994)
3. *Lemony Snicket's A Series of Unfortunate Events* (2004)

FORTY CHARACTERS

4. *The Lord of the Rings: The Fellowship of the Ring* (2001)

6 Shortest Oscar-Nominated Feature Films

Despite their abbreviated running times, all of these movies were nominated in Oscar categories for *feature films*, putting them up against much longer competitors. Consider that the first one on the list is a six-minute Woody Woodpecker cartoon that was nominated for Original Song against four movies that averaged ninety-three minutes in length.

Numbers three through six on the list were also nominated for their music, but number two is an exception: *The Red Balloon* (1956) actually *won* the Oscar in a feature-length category—Best Writing (Original Screenplay)— despite being barely a half-hour long. Just missing the cut are Walt Disney's *Dumbo* (1941) at sixty-four minutes and Mae West's *She Done Him Wrong* (1933) at sixty-six minutes (hers is still the shortest Best Picture nominee ever).

Note that most of the following movies were made in the 1930s and '40s, back when Hollywood often cranked 'em out short and fast. The average movie length in the 1930s was about ninety minutes, whereas now it's closer to two hours.

SIX MINUTES

1. *Wet Blanket Policy* (1948)

THIRTY-FOUR MINUTES

2. *The Red Balloon* (1956)

FORTY-SIX MINUTES

3. *Flying with Music* (1942)

FORTY-NINE MINUTES

4. *All-American Co-Ed* (1941)

FIFTY-SEVEN MINUTES

5. *Block-Heads* (1938)

SIXTY-ONE MINUTES

6. *Way Down South* (1939)

Gone with the Hour Hand: 10 Longest Oscar-Nominated Movies

Plenty of great Oscar-nominated and Oscar-winning movies are just over 180 minutes (three hours) long: *The Godfather* (1972) and *Schindler's List* (1993), to name two examples. A few more classics bust the deuce with runtimes over two hundred minutes, including *Giant* (1956) and *The Irishman* (2019). These next ten movies, however, are the longest Oscar nominees (and Oscar winners) ever, with two of them blasting past 420 minutes (that's over *seven* hours of a single movie). For some viewers, these behemoths may be hard to sit through, but for many others, they're harder to ignore.

There are different versions (some shorter, some longer) of some of the following movies, but we're using the lengths during their original releases. Additionally, the lengths (in minutes) are for the movies themselves without the inclusion of musical overtures, intermissions, *entr'acte* music, and concluding "exit music"; adding all those elements to the ninth movie on the list would lengthen the whole experience by about seventeen minutes, which is a lot of time gone with *Gone with the Wind*.

467 MINUTES

1. *O.J.: Made in America* (2016)

431 MINUTES

2. *War and Peace* (1968)

357 MINUTES

3. *Little Dorrit* (1987)

307 MINUTES

4. *The Deluge* (1974)

260 MINUTES

5. *The Greatest Story Ever Told* (1965)

248 MINUTES

6. *Cleopatra* (1963)

242 MINUTES

7. *Hamlet* (1996)

222 MINUTES

8. *Lawrence of Arabia* (1962)

221 MINUTES

9. *Gone with the Wind* (1939)

220 MINUTES

10. *The Ten Commandments* (1956)

10 Times When There Have Been Ties Between Multiple Winners

Typically one person, or one group representing a single movie, is announced as the winner for each Oscar category. But not always. These ten ceremonies featured ties between different movies in a single category, which meant co-winners, co-co-co-co-winners, and in one case co-co-co-co-co-co-co-winners. Imagine that impressive parade of seven separate winners to the stage . . . the big cluster of people around the podium . . . the array of glittering statuettes . . . and the acceptance speeches . . . the acceptance speeches . . . the acceptance speeches . . .

SEVEN WINNERS

1. Sixth ceremony (held in 1934)
Best Assistant Director
- Charles Barton, Charles Dorian, Dewey Starkey, Fred Fox, Gordon Hollingshead, Scott R. Beal, and William Tummel (winners and their studios were named, but not specific movies)

FOUR WINNERS

2. Fifteenth ceremony (held in 1943)

Best Documentary
- *The Battle of Midway* (1942)
- *Kokoda Front Line!* (1942)
- *Moscow Strikes Back* (1942)
- *Prelude to War* (1942)

TWO WINNERS

3. First ceremony (held in 1929)

Best Art Direction
- *The Dove* (1927)
- *Tempest* (1928)

4. Fifth ceremony (held in 1932)

Best Actor
- Wallace Beery, *The Champ* (1931)
- Fredric March, *Dr. Jekyll and Mr. Hyde* (1931)

5. Eighth ceremony (held in 1936)

Best Dance Direction
- *Broadway Melody of 1936* (1935)
- *Folies Bergère de Paris* (1935)

6. Twenty-second ceremony (held in 1950)

Best Documentary (Short Subject)
- *A Chance to Live* (1949)
- *So Much for So Little* (1949)

7. Forty-first ceremony (held in 1969)

Best Actress
- Katharine Hepburn, *The Lion in Winter* (1968)
- Barbra Streisand, *Funny Girl* (1968)

8. Fifty-ninth ceremony (held in 1986)

Best Documentary (Feature)
- *Artie Shaw: Time Is All You've Got* (1985)
- *Down and Out in America* (1986)

9. Sixty-seventh ceremony (held in 1995)

Best Short Film (Live Action)
- *Franz Kafka's It's a Wonderful Life* (1993)
- *Trevor* (1994)

10. Eighty-fifth ceremony (held in 2013)

Best Sound Editing
- *Skyfall* (2012)
- *Zero Dark Thirty* (2012)

You Can't Take All the Oscars with You: 4 Times When All Six Top Oscars Were Won by Six Different Movies

Indulge the notion that the "top Oscars" are defined as Best Picture, Best Actor, Best Actress, Best Supporting Actor, Best Supporting Actress, and Best Director, and you can then acknowledge that there were four Academy Awards ceremonies when all six Oscars went to six different movies. Incidentally, no one movie has ever swept all six of these "top Oscars." *You Can't Take It with You* (1938), the movie invoked in the subhead for this list, won two of the six, Best Picture and Best Director.

1. Twenty-fifth ceremony (held in 1953)

- Best Picture: *The Greatest Show on Earth* (1952)
- Best Actor: Gary Cooper, *High Noon* (1952)
- Best Actress: Shirley Booth, *Come Back, Little Sheba* (1952)
- Best Supporting Actor: Anthony Quinn, *Viva Zapata!* (1952)

- Best Supporting Actress: Gloria Grahame, *The Bad and the Beautiful* (1952)
- Best Director: John Ford, *The Quiet Man* (1952)

2. Twenty-ninth ceremony (held in 1957)

- Best Picture: *Around the World in 80 Days* (1956)
- Best Actor: *Yul Brynner, The King and I* (1956)
- Best Actress: Ingrid Bergman, *Anastasia* (1956)
- Best Supporting Actor: Anthony Quinn, *Lust for Life* (1956)
- Best Supporting Actress: Dorothy Malone, *Written on the Wind* (1956)
- Best Director: George Stevens, *Giant* (1956)

3. Seventy-eighth ceremony (held in 2006)

- Best Picture: *Crash* (2004)
- Best Actor: Philip Seymour Hoffman, *Capote* (2005)
- Best Actress: Reese Witherspoon, *Walk the Line* (2005)
- Best Supporting Actor: George Clooney, *Syriana* (2005)
- Best Supporting Actress: Rachel Weisz, *The Constant Gardener* (2005)
- Best Director: Ang Lee, *Brokeback Mountain* (2005)

4. Eighty-fifth ceremony (held in 2013)

- Best Picture: *Argo* (2012)
- Best Actor: Daniel Day-Lewis, *Lincoln* (2012)
- Best Actress: Jennifer Lawrence, *Silver Linings Playbook* (2012)
- Best Supporting Actor: Christoph Waltz, *Django Unchained* (2012)
- Best Supporting Actress: Anne Hathaway, *Les Misérables* (2012)
- Best Director: Ang Lee, *Life of Pi* (2012)

5 Ceremonies When a Movie Broke the Record for Most Oscar Wins

In the early years of the Academy Awards ceremonies, it wasn't uncommon for the night's big winner to have a total of only two or three wins. In fact, at the second ceremony (held in 1930 to celebrate movies from 1928 and '29), no movie won more than a single Oscar. Of course, there were far fewer categories back then (only seven at that second ceremony—seven categories, seven different winning movies), and thus fewer opportunities for a movie to win multiple Oscars.

Records, like the traffic laws in *The French Connection* (1971), were made to be broken. Accordingly, the record for most Oscar wins by a movie has progressed over the decades from three wins at the first ceremony to five wins, then to eight, nine, and eleven. The eleven Oscars won by *Ben-Hur* (1959) were later matched by *Titanic* (1997) and *The Lord of the Rings: The Return of the King* (2003), but no movie has ever surpassed that total. Here then, listed chronologically so you can chart the progress of the record, are the first ceremonies when movies had . . .

THREE WINS

1. First ceremony (held in 1929)

- *7th Heaven* (1927)
- *Sunrise* (1927)

FIVE WINS

2. Seventh ceremony (held in 1935)

- *It Happened One Night* (1934)

EIGHT WINS

3. Twelfth ceremony (held in 1940)

- *Gone with the Wind* (1939)

NINE WINS

4. Thirty-first ceremony (held in 1959)

- *Gigi* (1958)

ELEVEN WINS

5. Thirty-second ceremony (held in 1960)

- *Ben-Hur* (1959)

30 Movies with at Least Twelve Oscar Nominations

The movies with a dozen or more Oscar nominations almost constitute a "greatest hits" list of movie history. Just over half of the movies shown below went on to win Best Picture, which indicates that having a lot of nominations doesn't guarantee winning the top prize.

This point would be even stronger had we opened up the list to movies with ten or more nominations: that list of double-digit nominees would be *ninety-seven* movies long, with well under half—only forty-one of the ninety-seven—winning for Best Picture. Of the thirty movies listed below, movies within each grouping are listed in chronological order, and Best Picture winners are marked **Winner**.

FOURTEEN NOMINATIONS

1. **Winner** *All About Eve* (1950)
2. **Winner** *Titanic* (1997)
3. *La La Land* (2016)

THIRTEEN NOMINATIONS

4. **Winner** *Gone with the Wind* (1939)
5. **Winner** *From Here to Eternity* (1953)
6. *Mary Poppins* (1964)
7. *Who's Afraid of Virginia Woolf?* (1966)
8. **Winner** *Forrest Gump* (1994)
9. **Winner** *Shakespeare in Love* (1998)
10. *The Lord of the Rings: The Fellowship of the Ring* (2001)
11. **Winner** *Chicago* (2002)
12. *The Curious Case of Benjamin Button* (2008)
13. **Winner** *The Shape of Water* (2017)

TWELVE NOMINATIONS

14. Winner *Mrs. Miniver* (1942)

15. *The Song of Bernadette* (1943)

16. *Johnny Belinda* (1948)

17. *A Streetcar Named Desire* (1951)

18. Winner *On the Waterfront* (1954)

19. Winner *Ben-Hur* (1959)

20. *Becket* (1964)

21. Winner *My Fair Lady* (1964)

22. *Reds* (1981)

23. Winner *Dances with Wolves* (1990)

24. Winner *Schindler's List* (1993)

25. Winner *The English Patient* (1996)

The English Patient (1996).

26. Winner *Gladiator* (2000)

27. Winner *The King's Speech* (2010)

28. *Lincoln* (2012)

29. *The Revenant* (2015)

30. *The Power of the Dog* (2021)

4 Movies with Double-Digit Oscar Wins

Considering all the movies that have had double-digit Oscar nominations (see the previous list), surprisingly few movies have had double-digit Oscar wins. The fab four are listed below chronologically. Look up the word "classic" in the dictionary, and their posters might be illustrating the definition.

ELEVEN WINS

1. *Ben-Hur* (1959)
2. *Titanic* (1997)
3. *The Lord of the Rings: The Return of the King* (2003)

TEN WINS

4. *West Side Story* (1961)

100 Memorable Movies with Zero Oscar Nominations

Every movie fan could create a list like this one, because we've all got personal favorites that never received Oscar recognition. In our following list of familiar, occasionally great, and even revered movies, some of the conspicuous Oscar omissions seem baffling. *Gilda* (1946), which put Rita Hayworth in one of the most iconic dresses in movie history, couldn't get a simple nomination for Best Costume Design. Or consider *Help!* (1965), which has one of the best non-nominated movie theme songs ever. And what's with the missing nominations for the screenplay of *Sweet Smell of Success* (1957), the cinematography for *The Shining* (1980), and the visual effects in *The Dark Knight Rises* (2012)? You could present an awesome film festival drawn just from the non-nominees in the next list.

Undoubtedly some of the movies listed below alphabetically would have been nominated had every current Oscar category always existed. For instance, *Frankenstein* (1931), with its iconic monster design, would have been a certain nominee had there been a Best Makeup category at the time (that category wasn't launched until 1982). Similarly, *The Invisible Man* (1933) and *Snow White and the Seven Dwarfs* (1937) would've been unbeatable candidates if today's categories for Best Visual Effects and Best Animated Feature Film, respectively, had existed back then. For more frustrations over Oscar's non-nominees, see the list called "100 Memorable Movies That Didn't Get Nominated for Best Picture" on page 152.

100 Memorable Movies with Zero Oscar Nominations (Year)	
1. *Advise & Consent* (1962)	7. *The Big Sleep* (1946)
2. *Badlands* (1973)	8. *Blood Simple* (1984)
3. *Before Sunrise* (1995)	9. *The Breakfast Club* (1985)
4. *The Big Heat* (1953)	10. *Breathless* (1960)
5. *The Big Lebowski* (1998)	11. *Bringing Up Baby* (1938)
6. *The Big Red One* (1980)	12. *A Bronx Tale* (1993)

13. *Catch-22* (1970)	**42.** *Help!* (1965)
14. *A Christmas Story* (1983)	**43.** *High Sierra* (1941)
15. *City Lights* (1931)	**44.** *His Girl Friday* (1940)
16. *Coma* (1978)	**45.** *In a Lonely Place* (1950)
17. *Compulsion* (1959)	**46.** *The Invisible Man* (1933)
18. *The Dark Knight Rises* (2012)	**47.** *Jeremiah Johnson* (1972)
19. *The Day the Earth Stood Still* (1951)	**48.** *Johnny Guitar* (1954)
20. *Dead Ringers* (1988)	**49.** *Kill Bill: Volume One* (2003)
21. *Deadpool* (2016)	**50.** *Kill Bill: Volume Two* (2004)
22. *Dial M for Murder* (1954)	**51.** *The Killing* (1956)
23. *Dracula* (1931)	**52.** *King Kong* (1933)
24. *Drugstore Cowboy* (1989)	**53.** *The Lady from Shanghai* (1947)
25. *Duck Soup* (1933)	**54.** *The Lady Vanishes* (1938)
26. *Escape from Alcatraz* (1979)	**55.** *A League of Their Own* (1992)
27. *A Face in the Crowd* (1957)	**56.** *Lonely are the Brave* (1962)
28. *Fail Safe* (1964)	**57.** *Love and Death* (1975)
29. *Fantasia* (1940)	**58.** *M* (1931)
30. *Frankenstein* (1931)	**59.** *Mean Streets* (1973)
31. *The French Dispatch* (2021)	**60.** *Moby Dick* (1956)
32. *Fruitvale Station* (2013)	**61.** *Miller's Crossing* (1990)
33. *Get Shorty* (1995)	**62.** *Much Ado About Nothing* (1993)
34. *The Getaway* (1972)	**63.** *Murder, My Sweet* (1944)
35. *Gilda* (1946)	**64.** *My Darling Clementine* (1946)
36. *The Good, the Bad, and the Ugly* (1966)	**65.** *A Night at the Opera* (1935)
37. *The Great Waldo Pepper* (1975)	**66.** *The Night of the Hunter* (1955)
38. *Groundhog Day* (1993)	**67.** *A Night to Remember* (1958)
39. *Harold and Maude* (1971)	**68.** *Nightmare Alley* (1947)
40. *The Haunting* (1963)	**69.** *Once Upon a Time in America* (1984)
41. *Heat* (1995)	**70.** *Once Upon a Time in the West* (1968)

71. *Out of the Past* (1947)	**86.** *Sin City* (2005)
72. *Paths of Glory* (1957)	**87.** *Sullivan's Travels* (1941)
73. *Play It Again, Sam* (1972)	**88.** *Sweet Smell of Success* (1957)
74. *The Postman Always Rings Twice* (1946)	**89.** *The Taking of Pelham One Two Three* (1974)
75. *Reservoir Dogs* (1992)	**90.** *This Is Spinal Tap* (1984)
76. *The Roaring Twenties* (1939)	**91.** *3:10 to Yuma* (1957)
77. *Rope* (1948)	**92.** *To Have and Have Not* (1944)
78. *Roxanne* (1987)	**93.** *Touch of Evil* (1958)
79. *Rushmore* (1998)	**94.** *Trouble in Paradise* (1932)
80. *Russian Ark* (2002)	**95.** *Twentieth Century* (1934)
81. *Scarface* (1983)	**96.** *Westworld* (1973)
82. *The Searchers* (1956)	**97.** *What's Up, Doc?* (1972)
83. *Se7en* (1995)	**98.** *The Wild One* (1953)
84. *The Shining* (1980)	**99.** *The Women* (1939)
85. *The Shop Around the Corner* (1940)	**100.** *Zodiac* (2007)

The Greatest Shows on Earth: 8 Greatest Movies of All Time

To qualify for this next list, a movie had to meet four criteria. First it had to be a Best Picture winner. Second and third, it had to have the most Oscar nominations and the most wins of any movie that year. And finally, it had to have been the year's top-grossing, i.e. most popular, movie (according to the box-office specialists at the-numbers.com). The four criteria generated only eight movies that combined the Academy's overwhelming acclaim together with the public's enthusiastic reception to create what could legitimately be called the Greatest Movies of All Time.

Several movies came close by dominating every criteria but one. Here are three examples from different decades: *It Happened One Night* (1934) won Best Picture and the most Oscars, plus it was

1934's top ticket-seller, but *One Night of Love* (1934) had one more nomination. *The Godfather* (1972), the Best Picture winner and the year's box-office champ, tied *Cabaret* (1972) for most nominations (ten) but won only three Oscars to *Cabaret*'s eight. *Gandhi* (1982) won Best Picture and had the most nominations and wins, but it was far behind *E.T. the Extra-Terrestrial* (1982) in ticket sales. These and other great near-misses show that most times you can't have everything, though often you can have *almost* everything. The next eight movies, however, swept all four of our criteria and achieved Hollywood's ultimate ideal of great movies making great money. So put your hands together, people, and give it up for Hollywood's G.M.O.A.T.

LISTED CHRONOLOGICALLY

1. *Gone with the Wind* (1939)
2. *Going My Way* (1944)
3. *Ben-Hur* (1959)
4. *Lawrence of Arabia* (1962)
5. *The Sound of Music* (1965)
6. *Rain Man* (1988)
7. *Titanic* (1997)
8. *The Lord of the Rings: The Return of the King* (2003)

RANKED BY COMBINED OSCAR NOMINATIONS AND WINS

1. ***Titanic* (1997)**
   - 14 Oscar nominations + 11 Oscar wins = 25 total
2. ***Ben-Hur* (1959)**
   - 12 noms + 11 wins = 23 total
3. ***The Lord of the Rings: The Return of the King* (2003)**
   - 11 noms + 11 wins = 22 total

4. ***Gone with the Wind* (1939)**
- 13 noms + 8 wins = 21 total
5. ***Going My Way* (1944)**
- 10 noms + 7 wins = 17 total
6. ***Lawrence of Arabia* (1962)**
- 10 noms + 7 wins = 17 total
7. ***The Sound of Music* (1965)**
- 10 noms + 5 wins, both tied with *Doctor Zhivago* (1965) = 15 total
8. ***Rain Man* (1988)**
- 8 noms + 4 wins = 12 total

OSCAR-WINNING AND OSCAR-NOMINATED PEOPLE IN GENERAL

Extraordinary People: 7 People with at Least Eight Oscar Wins

A costume designer, two producers, two composers, and two art directors populate this list of seven movie-making legends who won at least eight competitive Oscars. Six-time winner Billy Wilder and five-timers Francis Ford Coppola and John Williams are among those who just missed the cut.

We're only counting competitive Oscars here; had we added in various "special awards" (such as the Jean Hersholt Humanitarian Award), the numbers would jump upwards for some of these Hollywood legends. For example, Walt Disney, shown below at number one, also received four non-competitive "special awards" in addition to his twenty-two competitive Oscars. Everybody's first and last Oscars are included to show the span of these amazing careers.

TWENTY-TWO WINS

1. Walt Disney

- Best Short Subject (Cartoon): *Flowers and Trees* (1932)
- Best Short Subject (Cartoon): *Winnie the Pooh and the Blustery Day* (1968)

ELEVEN WINS

2. Cedric Gibbons

- Best Art Direction: *The Bridge of San Luis Rey* (1929)
- Best Art Direction (Black-and-White): *Somebody Up There Likes Me* (1956)

NINE WINS

3. Alfred Newman

- Best Music (Scoring): *Alexander's Ragtime Band* (1938)
- Best Music (Scoring of Music—Adaptation or Treatment): *Camelot* (1967)

EIGHT WINS

4. Edith Head

- Best Costume Design (Black-and-White): *The Heiress* (1949)
- Best Costume Design: *The Sting* (1973)

5. Fred Quimby

- Best Short Subject (Cartoon): *The Milky Way* (1940)
- Best Short Subject (Cartoon): *Johann Mouse* (1953)

6. Alan Menken

- Best Music (Original Score): *The Little Mermaid* (1989)
- Best Music (Original Song): *Pocahontas* (1995)

7. Edwin B. Willis

- Best Art Direction (Color): *Blossoms in the Dust* (1941)
- Best Art Direction (Black-and-White): *Somebody Up There Likes Me* (1956)

6 People with at Least Thirty-Two Oscar Nominations

Quick, name people with over thirty Oscar nominations. Walt Disney, obviously; composer John Williams, definitely; and Edith Head, probably, she has to be up there somewhere. Well, actually an all-star team of a half-dozen people have earned at least thirty Oscar nominations. Had we extended this list to people with twenty or more nominations, we'd have added another twenty names, among them Woody Allen, Randy Newman, Meryl Streep, and Billy Wilder.

Shown below are true legends in their fields, plus their total nominations for competitive Oscars. We've included everybody's first and last Oscar nominations so you can fully appreciate their longevity, and **Winner** marks a nomination that resulted in a win. Throughout the list we've used the specific name for each category as it was used in that particular year. Be sure to appreciate the greatness of John Williams, the only person on the list with nominations spanning *seven* decades, and as of 2023 the oldest nominee ever (90).

FIFTY-NINE NOMINATIONS

1. Walt Disney

- Best Short Subject (Cartoon): *Mickey's Orphans* (1931)
- **Winner** Best Short Subject (Cartoon): *Winnie the Pooh and the Blustery Day* (1968)

FIFTY-THREE NOMINATIONS

2. John Williams

- Best Music (Scoring of Music—Adaptation or Treatment): *Valley of the Dolls* (1967)
- Best Music (Original Score): *The Fabelmans* (2022)

FORTY-FIVE NOMINATIONS

3. Alfred Newman

- Best Music (Score): *The Prisoner of Zenda* (1937)
- Best Music (Original Score): *Airport* (1970)

THIRTY-NINE NOMINATIONS

4. Cedric Gibbons

- **Winner** Best Art Direction: *The Bridge of San Luis Rey* (1929)
- **Winner** Best Art Direction (Black-and-White): *Somebody Up There Likes Me* (1956)

THIRTY-FIVE NOMINATIONS

5. Edith Head

- Best Costume Design (Color): *The Emperor Waltz* (1948)
- Best Costume Design: *Airport '77* (1977)

THIRTY-TWO NOMINATIONS

6. Edwin B. Willis

- Best Art Direction: *Romeo and Juliet* (1936)
- Best Art Direction: *Les Girls* (1957)

Nothing Nowhere Not All at Once: 9 People with at Least Twelve Oscar Nominations and Zero Wins

"It's an honor just to be nominated," they say. If that's true, then Federico Fellini must have felt very honored, because he made this list of nominees who were up for Oscars a dozen or more times without once taking home a statuette. Among those who came close to making the list are director Ingmar Bergman, composer James Newton Howard, and director Stanley Kramer. Diane Warren at number five and Daniel Sudick at number seven are the two most recent additions.

Only competitive Oscars are being considered here, not any other special tributes; Fellini, for example, received an Honorary Award in 1992, and Loren L. Ryder right below him received *eight* technical, honorary, and other "special awards" (Ryder also had an impressive streak of competitive nominations at *nine* ceremonies in a row). Below each name is the most recent movie the person was nominated for.

SIXTEEN NOMINATIONS

1. Greg P. Russell

- Best Sound Mixing: *Skyfall* (2012)

FIFTEEN NOMINATIONS

2. Roland Anderson

- Art Direction (Color): *Come Blow Your Horn* (1963)

FOURTEEN NOMINATIONS

3. Thomas Newman

- Best Music (Original Score): *1917* (2019)

4. Alex North

- Best Music (Original Score): *Under the Volcano* (1984)

5. Diane Warren

- Best Music (Original Song): *Tell It Like a Woman* (2022)

THIRTEEN NOMINATIONS

6. George J. Folsey

- Best Cinematography (Black-and-White): *The Balcony* (1963)

7. Daniel Sudick

- Best Visual Effects: *Black Panther: Wakanda Forever* (2022)

TWELVE NOMINATIONS

8. Federico Fellini

- Best Writing (Screenplay—Based on Material from Another Medium): *Fellini's Casanova* (1976)

9. Loren L. Ryder

- Best Sound Recording: *The Ten Commandments* (1956)

10 Times Someone Had at Least Four Nominations at One Oscar Ceremony

Imagine being nominated for not just one, two, or three Oscars at a single ceremony, but being nominated for *four* or more. Good luck keeping your acceptance speeches straight if you win. And you probably *will* win, at least once, right? With four nominations, you'd think the odds are in your favor and you're certain to win something.

As Einstein said when he incorrectly wrote down $E=mc^3$, what could go wrong with this formula? Miscalculation, that's what, because unfortunately about half of the time that someone has four simultaneous nominations they don't win at all. Victor Young, shown below at numbers three and four, had an astonishing *eight* nominations in a two-year period, and didn't win for any of them. Note too that some of the people on the list were nominated for multiple movies at one ceremony, but a few—including the Coen brothers and Chloé Zhao— were nominated in four different categories for a single movie (these versatile filmmakers would probably hammer nails into the sets if they had the time). Winning nominations are marked **Winner** .

SIX NOMINATIONS

1. Twenty-sixth ceremony (held in 1954)

Walt Disney
- Best Short Subject (Cartoon): *Rugged Bear* (1953)
- **Winner** Best Short Subject (Cartoon): *Toot, Whistle, Plunk and Boom* (1953)
- **Winner** Best Short Subject (Two-Reel): *Bear Country* (1953)
- Best Short Subject (Two-Reel): *Ben and Me* (1953)
- **Winner** Best Documentary (Feature): *The Living Desert* (1953)
- **Winner** Best Documentary (Short Subject): *The Alaskan Eskimo* (1953)

FOUR NOMINATIONS

2. Eleventh ceremony (held in 1939)

Walt Disney
- Best Short Subject (Cartoon): *Brave Little Tailor* (1938)
- **Winner** Best Short Subject (Cartoon): *Ferdinand the Bull* (1938)
- Best Short Subject (Cartoon): *Good Scouts* (1938)
- Best Short Subject (Cartoon): *Mother Goose Goes Hollywood* (1938)

3. Twelfth ceremony (held in 1940)

Alfred Newman
- Best Music (Original Score): *The Rains Came* (1939)
- Best Music (Original Score): *Wuthering Heights* (1939)

- Best Music (Scoring): *The Hunchback of Notre Dame* (1939)
- Best Music (Scoring): *They Shall Have Music* (1939)

Victor Young
- Best Music (Original Score): *Golden Boy* (1939)
- Best Music (Original Score): *Gulliver's Travels* (1939)
- Best Music (Original Score): *Man of Conquest* (1939)
- Best Music (Scoring): *Way Down South* (1939)

4. Thirteenth ceremony (held in 1941)

Victor Young
- Best Music (Original Score): *Arizona* (1940)
- Best Music (Original Score): *Dark Command* (1940)
- Best Music (Original Score): *North West Mounted Police* (1940)
- Best Music (Scoring): *Arise, My Love* (1940)

5. Twenty-fourth ceremony (held in 1952)

Thomas Little and Lyle R. Wheeler
- Best Art Direction (Black-and-White): *Fourteen Hours* (1951)
- Best Art Direction (Black-and-White): *The House on Telegraph Hill* (1951)
- Best Art Direction (Color): *David and Bathsheba* (1951)
- Best Art Direction (Color): *On the Riviera* (1951)

6. Fifty-first ceremony (held in 1979)

Warren Beatty
- Best Actor; Best Director; Best Picture (Producer); Best Writing (Screenplay Based on Material from Another Medium): *Heaven Can Wait* (1978)

7. Fifty-fourth ceremony (held in 1982)

Warren Beatty

- Best Actor; **Winner** Best Director; Best Picture (Producer); Best Writing (Screenplay Written Directly for the Screen): *Reds* (1981)

8. Eightieth ceremony (held in 2008)

Ethan Coen and Joel Coen

- **Winner** Best Director; Best Film Editing; **Winner** Best Picture (Producers); **Winner** Best Writing (Adapted Screenplay): *No Country for Old Men* (2007)

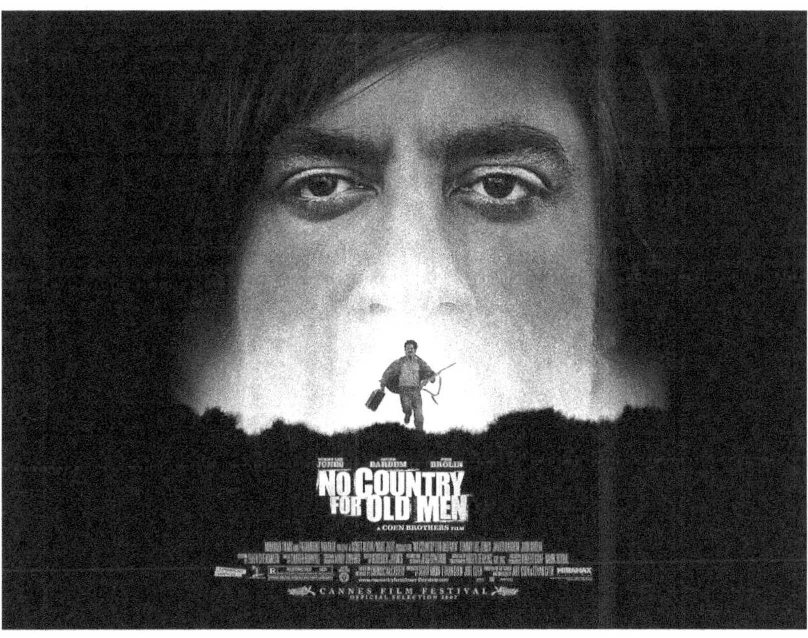

9. Ninety-first ceremony (held in 2019)

Alfonso Cuarón

- **Winner** Best Cinematography; **Winner** Best Director; Best Picture (Producer); Best Writing (Original Screenplay): *Roma* (2018)

10. Ninety-third ceremony (held in 2021)

Chloé Zhao
- **Winner** Best Director; Best Film Editing; **Winner** Best Picture (Producer); Best Writing (Adapted Screenplay): *Nomadland* (2020)

14 People Who Won at Least Three Oscars at One Oscar Ceremony

That Walt Disney was a dynamo. Just consider how he's dominated all of these recent lists for most career wins, most career nominations, and most nominations at a single Oscar ceremony. The man was basically an acceptance speech waiting to happen.

Another area where he's ahead of an elite pack: most Oscar wins at one ceremony, as shown below. One common misconception is that Bong Joon-ho tied Disney when *Parasite* (2019) won four Oscars at the ninety-second ceremony (held in 2020). Bong Joon-ho won three of them, and while he was at the podium to accept the fourth (Best International Feature Film), that award actually went to the country (South Korea), not specifically to him. Incidentally, the first person to claim two Oscars at one ceremony was William Cameron Menzies, a Best Art Direction double-winner for *The Dove* (1927) and *Tempest* (1928) at the first Oscar ceremony (held in 1929).

FOUR WINS

1. Walt Disney

Twenty-sixth ceremony (held in 1954)

- Best Short Subject (Cartoon): *Toot, Whistle, Plunk and Boom* (1953)
- Best Short Subject (Two-Reel): *Bear Country* (1953)
- Best Documentary (Feature): *The Living Desert* (1953)
- Best Documentary (Short Subject): *The Alaskan Eskimo* (1953)

THREE WINS

2. Bong Joon-ho

Ninety-second ceremony (held in 2020)
- Best Director; Best Picture (Producer); Best Writing (Original Screenplay): *Parasite* (2019)

Parasite (2019).

3. James L. Brooks

Fifty-sixth ceremony (held in 1984)
- Best Director; Best Picture (Producer); Best Writing (Screenplay Based on Material from Another Medium): *Terms of Endearment* (1983)

4. James Cameron

Seventieth ceremony (held in 1998)
- Best Director; Best Film Editing; Best Picture (Producer): *Titanic* (1997)

5.-6. Ethan Coen and Joel Coen

Eightieth ceremony (held in 2008)
- Best Director; Best Picture (Producer); Best Writing (Adapted Screenplay): *No Country for Old Men* (2007)

7. Francis Ford Coppola

Forty-seventh ceremony (held in 1975)
- Best Director; Best Picture (Producer); Best Writing (Screenplay Adapted from Other Material): *The Godfather: Part II* (1974)

8. Marvin Hamlisch

Forty-sixth ceremony (held in 1974)
- Best Music (Original Dramatic Score) and Best Music (Song): *The Way We Were* (1973)
- Best Music (Scoring: Original Song Score and Adaptation—or—Scoring: Adaptation): *The Sting* (1973)

9. Alejandro G. Iñárritu

Eighty-seventh ceremony (held in 2015)
- Best Director; Best Picture (Producer); Best Writing (Original Screenplay): *Birdman or (The Unexpected Virtue of Ignorance)* (2014)

10. Peter Jackson

Seventy-sixth ceremony (held in 2004)
- Best Director; Best Picture (Producer); Best Writing (Adapted Screenplay): *The Lord of the Rings: The Return of the King* (2003)

11.-12. Daniel Kwan and Daniel Scheinert

Ninety-fifth ceremony (held in 2023)
- Best Director; Best Picture (Producer); Best Writing (Original Screenplay): *Everything Everywhere All at Once* (2007)

13. Fran Walsh

Seventy-sixth ceremony (held in 2004)
- Best Music (Original Song); Best Picture (Producer); Best Writing (Adapted Screenplay): *The Lord of the Rings: The Return of the King* (2003)

14. Billy Wilder

Thirty-third ceremony (held in 1961)
- Best Director; Best Picture (Producer); Best Writing (Story and Screenplay—Written Directly for the Screen): *The Apartment* (1960)

4 People Nominated in at Least Six Different Categories

Bet you can't guess who the co-leaders of this next list are. They would have to be polymaths who excelled in a half-dozen movie-making fields, right? So, Walt Disney perhaps? Makes sense, since he has the most nominations in history. Disney's close, but actually he's tied for second. The leaders are still working and didn't separate themselves from the others until recent years, when they both got their seventh nominations. Under each of the following names are the first nominations in the different categories, presented in chronological order with wins noted.

SEVEN DIFFERENT CATEGORIES

1. Kenneth Branagh

- Best Actor: *Henry V* (1989)
- Best Director: *Henry V* (1989)
- Best Short Film (Live Action): *Swan Song* (1992)
- Best Writing (Screenplay Based on Material Previously Produced or Published): *Hamlet* (1996)
- Best Supporting Actor: *My Week with Marilyn* (2011)
- Best Picture (Producer): *Belfast* (2021)
- **Winner** Best Writing (Original Screenplay): *Belfast* (2021)

2. Alfonso Cuarón

- Best Writing (Original Screenplay): *Y Tu Mamá También* (2001)
- Best Film Editing: *Children of Men* (2006)
- Best Writing (Adapted Screenplay): *Children of Men* (2006)
- **Winner** Best Director: *Gravity* (2013)
- Best Picture (Producer): *Gravity* (2013)
- **Winner** Best Cinematography: *Roma* (2018)
- Best Short Film (Live Action): *Le Pupille* (2022)

SIX DIFFERENT CATEGORIES

3. George Clooney

- **Winner** Best Supporting Actor: *Syriana* (2005)
- Best Director: *Good Night, and Good Luck.* (2005)
- Best Writing (Original Screenplay): *Good Night, and Good Luck.* (2005)

- Best Actor: *Michael Clayton* (2007)
- Best Writing (Adapted Screenplay): *The Ides of March* (2011)
- **Winner** Best Picture (Producer): *Argo* (2012)

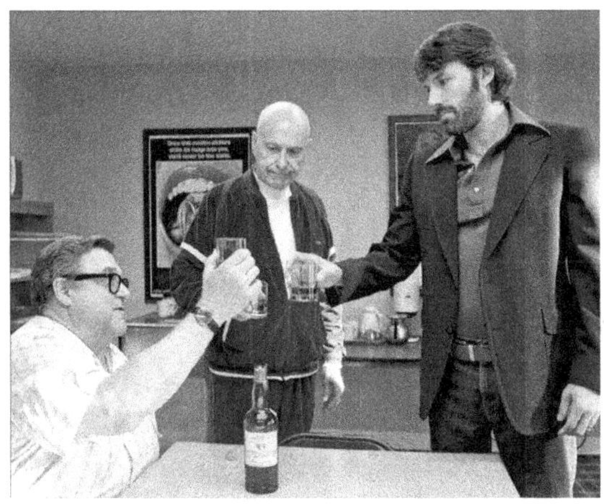

Argo (2012).

4. Walt Disney

- **Winner** Best Short Subject (Cartoon): *Flowers and Trees* (1932)
- Best Documentary: *The Grain That Built a Hemisphere* (1943)
- Best Short Subject (Two-Reel): *Seal Island* (1948)
- **Winner** Best Documentary (Short Subject): *The Alaskan Eskimo* (1953)
- **Winner** Best Short Subject (Live Action): *Grand Canyon* (1958)
- Best Picture (Producer): *Mary Poppins* (1964)

3 Longest Streaks of Consecutive Oscar Wins

Winning one Oscar is difficult; winning two is rare; winning three, rarer still. So consider the amazing achievements of the following people who not only won four or more Oscars but won them *consecutively*. Imagine that, winning an Oscar four, six, or eight years in a row (costume designer Edith Head is in the larger group, not shown here, that won Oscars at three consecutive ceremonies).

During these incredible streaks each person had additional nominations: Thomas Little had eight nominations overall during his four-year run of wins, while Walt Disney had *fifteen* nominations overall during his eight-year winning streak as the producer of memorable cartoons. The winning movies that started and ended each streak are shown.

EIGHT YEARS IN A ROW

1. Walt Disney

Fifth ceremony (held in 1932) to twelfth ceremony (held in 1940)
- Best Short Subject (Cartoon): *Flowers and Trees* (1932)
- Best Short Subject (Cartoon): *The Ugly Duckling* (1939)

SIX YEARS IN A ROW

2. Walt Disney

Twenty-third ceremony (held in 1951) to twenty-eighth ceremony (held in 1956)
- Best Short Subject (Two-Reel): *Beaver Valley* (1950)
- Best Documentary (Short Subject): *Men Against the Arctic* (1955)

FOUR YEARS IN A ROW

3. Thomas Little

Fourteenth ceremony (held in 1942) to seventeenth ceremony (held in 1945)
- Best Art Direction (Black-and-White): *How Green Was My Valley* (1941)
- Best Art Direction (Color): *Wilson* (1944)

15 Posthumous Oscar Winners

Sadly, some Oscar winners weren't alive to receive the Academy's acknowledgement of their cinematic efforts. This next list presents fifteen alphabetical examples of posthumous award winners in competitive Oscar categories.

We're only focusing on Oscar winners here, not the scores of posthumous *nominees* who would've dramatically expanded the list, including famous names like actors James Dean and Spencer Tracy, and composers George Gershwin and Bernard Herrmann. We also haven't included the blacklisted writers Carl Foreman, Dalton Trumbo, and Michael Wilson, who were presented with posthumous Oscars after the Academy revised its records. See the list called "It Happened One Oscar Night: 17 Controversial Oscar Wins and Nominations" on page 77 for more on these three writers.

1. Howard Ashman

- Best Music (Original Song): *Beauty and the Beast* (1991)

2. Walt Disney

- Best Short Film (Cartoon): *Winnie the Pooh and the Blustery Day* (1968)

3. Peter Finch

- Best Actor: *Network* (1976)

4. Gil Friesen

- Best Documentary (Feature): *20 Feet from Stardom* (2013)

5. Thomas C. Goodwin

- Best Documentary (Short Subject): *Educating Peter* (1992)

6. Conrad Hall

- Best Cinematography: *Road to Perdition* (2002)

7. William A. Horning

- Best Art Direction: *Gigi* (1958)
- Best Art Direction (Color): *Ben-Hur* (1959)

8. Sidney Howard

- Best Writing (Screenplay): *Gone with the Wind* (1939)

9. Heath Ledger

- Best Supporting Actor: *The Dark Knight* (2008)

10. Eric Orbom

- Best Art Direction (Color): *Spartacus* (1960)

11. Raymond Rasch

- Best Music (Original Dramatic Score): *Limelight* (1952)

12. Larry Russell

- Best Music (Original Dramatic Score): *Limelight* (1952)

13. Geoffrey Unsworth

- Best Cinematography: *Tess* (1979)

14. Victor Young

- Best Music (Music Score of a Dramatic or Comedy Picture): *Around the World in 80 Days* (1956)

15. Sam Zimbalist

- Best Picture (Producer): *Ben-Hur* (1959)

Mi Casablanca, Su Casablanca: 17 Pairs of Oscar-Winning Siblings

Occasionally brothers and sisters have both won competitive Oscars. Seventeen pairs of siblings are shown below, followed by their first Oscar-winning movies.

Since we're limiting the list to siblings who *both* won Oscars, another eleven pairs of siblings aren't included because one of the siblings was a nominee but not a winner. Those eleven pairs, with the Oscar-winning sibling listed ahead of the Oscar-nominated sibling: Woody Allen and Letty Aronson; Francis Ford Coppola and Talia Shire; Sofia Coppola and Roman Coppola; Jane Fonda and Peter Fonda; Anjelica Huston and Tony Huston; Gordon Jennings and Devereaux Jennings; Emil Newman, the only one of the three Newman brothers not to win an Oscar (the other two are listed below); Joaquin Phoenix and River Phoenix; Vanessa Redgrave and Lynn Redgrave; Julia Roberts and Eric Roberts; Steven Spielberg and Anne Spielberg. We could also mention two pairs of siblings where everybody got nominated and nobody won: Maggie and Jake Gyllenhaal, and Jennifer and Meg Tilly. In the following list, oldest sibs come first.

1. Affleck

Ben
- Best Picture (Producer): *Argo* (2012)

Casey
- Best Actor: *Manchester by the Sea* (2016)

2. Barrymore

Lionel
- Best Actor: *A Free Soul* (1931)

Ethel
- Best Supporting Actress: *None But the Lonely Heart* (1944)

3. Boekelheide

Jay
- Best Sound Effects Editing: *The Right Stuff* (1983)

Todd
- Best Sound: *Amadeus* (1984)

4. Coen

Joel
- Best Writing (Screenplay Written Directly for the Screen): *Fargo* (1996)

Ethan
- Best Writing (Screenplay Written Directly for the Screen): *Fargo* (1996)

5. Corbould

Chris
- Best Visual Effects: *Inception* (2010)

Neil
- Best Visual Effects: *Gladiator* (2000)

6. de Havilland and Fontaine

Olivia de Havilland
- Best Actress: *To Each His Own* (1946)

Joan Fontaine
- Best Actress: *Suspicion* (1941)

7. Epstein (twins)

Julius
- Best Writing (Screenplay): *Casablanca* (1942)

Philip
- Best Writing (Screenplay): *Casablanca* (1942)

8. Goldman

James
- Best Writing (Screenplay—Based on Material from Another Medium): *The Lion in Winter* (1968)

William
- Best Writing (Story and Screenplay—Based on Material Not Previously Published or Produced): *Butch Cassidy and the Sundance Kid* (1969)

9. Lauenstein (twins)

Christoph
- Best Short Film (Animated): *Balance* (1989)

Wolfgang
- Best Short Film (Animated): *Balance* (1989)

10. MacLaine and Beatty

Shirley MacLaine
- Best Actress: *Terms of Endearment* (1983)

Warren Beatty
- Best Director: *Reds* (1981)

11. Mankiewicz

Herman
- Best Writing (Original Screenplay): *Citizen Kane* (1941)

Joseph
- Best Director: *A Letter to Three Wives* (1949)

12. Newman

Alfred
- Best Music (Scoring): *Alexander's Ragtime Band* (1938)

Lionel
- Best Music (Score of a Musical Picture—Original or Adaptation): *Hello, Dolly!* (1969)

13. O'Connell and Eilish

Finneas O'Connell
- Best Music (Original Song): *No Time to Die* (2021)

Billie Eilish
- Best Music (Original Song): *No Time to Die* (2021)

14. Sanders

Denis
- Best Short Subject (Two-Reel): *A Time Out of War* (1954)

Terry
- Best Short Subject (Two-Reel): *A Time Out of War* (1954)

15. Shearer

Douglas
- Best Sound Recording: *The Big House* (1930)

Norma
- Best Actress: *The Divorcee* (1930)

16. Sherman

Robert
- Best Music (Song): *Mary Poppins* (1964)

Richard
- Best Music (Song): *Mary Poppins* (1964)

17. Sylbert (twins)

Paul
- Best Art Direction: *Heaven Can Wait* (1978)

Richard
- Best Art Direction (Black-and-White): *Who's Afraid of Virginia Woolf?* (1966)

18 Pairs of Oscar-Winning Parents and Children

Reinforcing what's shown in the previous list, this next one proves that sometimes Oscars run in the family, and what may have started with "take your kid to work day" culminated years later with two generations of Oscars. Eighteen pairs of Oscar-winning parents and their Oscar-winning children are shown below, along with their first Oscar-winning movies.

By limiting the list to a parent and a child who *both* won Oscars, another seven pairs of parents and children aren't included because one of the people in the pair was a nominee but not a winner. The special six: Oscar-winner Francis Ford Coppola and Oscar-nominee Roman Coppola; Oscar-nominee Bruce Dern/Oscar-nominee Diane Ladd and Oscar-winner Laura Dern; Oscar-nominee Kirk Douglas and Oscar-winner Michael Douglas; Oscar-winner Henry Fonda and Oscar-nominee Peter Fonda; Oscar-nominee Judy Garland and Oscar-winner Liza Minnelli; Oscar-nominee Tony Curtis/Oscar-nominee Janet Leigh and Oscar-winner Jamie Lee Curtis; and Oscar-winner George Stevens and Oscar-nominee George Stevens Jr. Throughout this paragraph and the following list, parents come first. Note how Francis Ford Coppola and John Huston each appear twice as the hinges in *three* generations of Oscar winners.

1. Berri and Langmann

Claude Berri
- Best Short Subject (Live Action): *Le Poulet* (1963)

Thomas Langmann
- Best Picture (Producer): *The Artist* (2011)

2. Bosustow

Stephen
- Best Short Subject (Cartoon): *Gerald McBoing-Boing* (1950)

Nick
- Best Short Subject (Cartoon): *Is It Always Right to Be Right?* (1970)

3. Coppola

Carmine
- Best Music (Original Dramatic Score): *The Godfather: Part II* (1974)

Francis Ford
- Best Writing (Story and Screenplay—Based on Factual Material or Material Not Previously Published or Produced): *Patton* (1970)

4. Coppola

Francis Ford
- Best Writing (Story and Screenplay—Based on Factual Material or Material Not Previously Published or Produced): *Patton* (1970)

Sofia
- Best Writing (Original Screenplay): *Lost in Translation* (2003)

5. Fisher

Thomas
- Best Visual Effects: *Titanic* (1997)

Scott
- Best Visual Effects: *Interstellar* (2014)

6. Fonda

Henry
- Best Actor: *On Golden Pond* (1981)

Jane
- Best Actress: *Klute* (1971)

7. George

Terry
- Best Short Film (Live Action): *The Shore* (2011)

Oorlagh
- Best Short Film (Live Action): *The Shore* (2011)

8. Guggenheim

Charles
- Best Short Subject (Live Action): *Robert Kennedy Remembered* (1968)

Davis
- Best Documentary (Feature): *An Inconvenient Truth* (2006)

9. Horner

Harry
- Best Art Direction (Black-and-White): *The Heiress* (1949)

James
- Best Music (Original Song): *Titanic* (1997)

10. Huston

Walter
- Best Supporting Actor: *The Treasure of the Sierra Madre* (1948)

John
- Best Director: *The Treasure of the Sierra Madre* (1948)

11. Huston

John
- Best Director: *The Treasure of the Sierra Madre* (1948)

Anjelica
- Best Supporting Actress: *Prizzi's Honor* (1985)

12. Kress

Harold
- Best Film Editing: *How the West Was Won* (1962)

Carl
- Best Film Editing: *The Towering Inferno* (1974)

13. Magnusson

Tivi
- Best Short Film (Live Action): *The New Tenants* (2009)

Kim
- Best Short Film (Live Action): *Valgaften* (1998)

14. Minnelli

Vincente
- Best Director: *Gigi* (1958)

Liza
- Best Actress: *Cabaret* (1972)

15. Rouse

Russell
- Best Writing (Story and Screenplay—Written Directly for the Screen): *Pillow Talk* (1959)

Christopher
- Best Film Editing: *The Bourne Ultimatum* (2007)

16. Voight and Jolie

Jon Voight
- Best Actor: *Coming Home* (1978)

Angelina Jolie
- Best Supporting Actress: *Girl, Interrupted* (1999)

17. Warren

Gene
- Best Special Effects: *The Time Machine* (1960)

Gene Jr.
- Best Visual Effects: Terminator 2: *Judgment Day* (1991)

18. Zanuck

Darryl
- Best Picture (Producer): *All About Eve* (1950)

Richard

- Best Picture (Producer): *Driving Miss Daisy* (1989)

Bravehearts: 13 Pairs of Spouses Who Shared Oscars for the Same Movie

Many pairs of spouses have won Oscars for their work on separate movies. For example, Vivien Leigh and her husband Laurence Olivier, and Joanne Woodward and her husband Paul Newman, all won Oscars, but they won in different categories (Best Actress and Best Actor) and for different movies. Occasionally, however, both spouses in a married couple have won the *same* Oscar in the *same* category for the *same* movie.

Here is a baker's dozen of alphabetically listed couples, their shared categories, and their first shared movies that won Oscars. Only feature films are included here; had we included short documentaries and short animated movies, the list would've been almost twice as long.

1. Edward and Edna Anhalt

- Best Writing (Motion Picture Story): *Panic in the Streets* (1950)

2. Alan and Marilyn Bergman

- Best Music (Original Song): *The Thomas Crown Affair* (1968)

3. Sydney and Muriel Box

- Best Writing (Screenplay): *The Seventh Veil* (1945)

4. Jimmy Chin and Elizabeth Chai Vasarhelyi

- Best Documentary (Feature): *Free Solo* (2018)

5. Dante Ferretti and Francesca Lo Schiavo

- Best Art Direction: *The Aviator* (2004)

6. Peter Jackson and Fran Walsh

- Best Picture (Producers): *The Lord of the Rings: The Return of the King* (2003)

7. Robert Lopez and Kristen Anderson-Lopez

- Best Music (Original Song): *Frozen* (2013)

8. Bob Murawski and Chris Innis

- Best Film Editing: *The Hurt Locker* (2008)

The Hurt Locker (2008).

9. Michael and Julia Phillips

- Best Picture (Producers): *The Sting* (1973)

10. Alan and Susan Raymond

- Best Documentary (Feature): *I Am a Promise: The Children of Stanton Elementary School* (1993)

11. Earl and Pamela Wallace

- Best Writing (Screenplay Written Directly for the Screen): *Witness* (1985)

12. David Wasco and Sandy Reynolds-Wasco

- Best Production Design: *La La Land* (2016)

13. Richard Zanuck and Lili Fini Zanuck

- Best Picture (Producers): *Driving Miss Daisy* (1989)

It Happened One Oscar Night: 17 Controversial Oscar Wins and Nominations

This list covers controversies involving the voting, the Oscar nominees, and the Oscar winners, not controversial events that occurred during the televised ceremonies (to read about 1974's infamous streaker, 2017's crazy Best Picture announcement, and other bizarre TV moments, see the list called "The Oddfather: 25 Awkward Moments at the Academy Awards Ceremony" on page 560). The following controversies are listed chronologically by the years of the ceremonies.

1. Eighth ceremony (held in 1936)

In 1936 screenwriter Dudley Nichols became the first winner to refuse to accept his Oscar. Nichols wanted to show his support for the Writers Guild, which was clashing with Hollywood studios and boycotting the ceremony.

- Best Writing (Screenplay): Dudley Nichols, *The Informer* (1935)

2. Ninth ceremony (held in 1937)

Spencer Tracy's Best Actor nomination turned heads, since he was in his movie for only about fifteen minutes. By comparison, Christoph Waltz later won in the *supporting* category with a *sixty-six* minute performance in *Django Unchained* (2012). Like Tracy, Hermione Baddeley was also recognized for an extremely brief appearance— two-and-a-half minutes in *Room at the Top* (1959), the shortest performance ever to earn a Best Supporting Actress nomination. Incidentally, Beatrice Straight gave the shortest performance, about five minutes in *Network* (1976), to actually win a Best Supporting Actress Oscar.

- Best Actor nominee: Spencer Tracy, *San Francisco* (1936)

3. Seventeenth ceremony (held in 1945)

For the first (and only) time someone was nominated in two different acting categories for playing one role. A voting loophole, which was quickly closed, enabled Barry Fitzgerald to be nominated as both Best Actor and Best Supporting Actor (he won for the latter).

- Best Supporting Actor: Barry Fitzgerald, *Going My Way* (1944)

4. Twenty-sixth ceremony (held in 1954)

Ian McLellan Hunter won a Best Writing Oscar at the twenty-sixth Oscar ceremony. Hunter turned out to be a "front" for blacklisted writer Dalton Trumbo, who had been identified as a Communist sympathizer and so wasn't allowed to work in Hollywood. Working with Trumbo, Hunter, himself an accomplished screenwriter, had submitted Trumbo's screenplay under his own name and handed the earnings to Trumbo. The Academy finally honored Trumbo with this posthumous Oscar in 1993.

- Best Writing (Motion Picture Story): Ian McLellan Hunter, later corrected to Dalton Trumbo, *Roman Holiday* (1953)

5. Twenty-ninth ceremony (held in 1957)

High Society (1955) is a sixty-one minute Bowery Boys comedy; *High Society* (1956) is a 111-minute musical starring Bing Crosby, Grace Kelly, and Frank Sinatra. Unfortunately, Academy voters accidentally nominated the screenplay for the 1955 comedy, not the 1956 musical as intended, for Best Writing (Motion Picture Story). Once the mistake was recognized, the 1955 screenwriters pulled their nomination from consideration before the ceremony. However, another controversy soon followed, because this category's winner was announced as Robert Rich, a name eventually revealed to be a pseudonym used by, ta da, Dalton Trumbo, the same black-listed screenwriter mentioned above. The Academy finally presented Trumbo this Oscar in 1976.

- Best Writing (Motion Picture Story): Robert Rich, later corrected to Dalton Trumbo, *The Brave One* (1956)

6. Thirtieth ceremony (held in 1958)

In 1952 Pierre Boulle wrote the French novel that became the Oscar-winning movie *The Bridge on the River Kwai* (1957). In 1958, Boulle was the Oscar winner for this movie's adapted screenplay, even though he hadn't written the screenplay and didn't even speak English. The two screenwriters who really did earn this Oscar, Carl Foreman and Michael Wilson, had been blacklisted as Communist sympathizers, making Boulle the de facto winner. The Academy awarded posthumous Oscars to Foreman and Wilson in 1984.

- Best Writing (Screenplay—Based on Material from Another Medium): Pierre Boulle, later corrected to Pierre Boulle, Carl Foreman and Michael Wilson, *The Bridge on the River Kwai* (1957)

7. Thirty-first ceremony (held in 1959)

Like Dalton Trumbo, Nedrick Young was a blacklisted writer who won an Oscar under a pseudonym—Nathan E. Douglas, the credited screenwriter of *The Defiant Ones* (1958). Young's widow finally received her husband's rightful Oscar in 1993.

- Best Writing (Story and Screenplay—Written Directly for the Screen): Nathan E. Douglas, later corrected to Nedrick Young, *The Defiant Ones* (1958)

8. Forty-first ceremony (held in 1969)

In 1969 *Young Americans* (1967) won for Best Documentary (Feature), but three weeks after the ceremony the Academy retracted that win because of a technicality. *Young Americans* was deemed ineligible because it had been released in 1967, and the 1969 ceremony was honoring 1968's movies. *Journey Into Self* (1968), the first runner-up in the voting, was named the winning documentary.

- Best Documentary (Feature): *Young Americans* (1967), later corrected to *Journey Into Self* (1968)

9. Forty-second ceremony (held in 1970)

The 1970 ceremony honored movies that had been made in 1969, which had been the first full year that rating symbols (G, M, R, and X) had been applied to movies. It didn't take long for the Academy to do something daring: *Midnight Cowboy* (1969) was the handy dynamite that immediately blasted open the doors to adult themes and became the first (and so far only) X-rated movie to win the Oscar for Best Picture.

- Best Picture: *Midnight Cowboy* (1969)

10. Forty-third ceremony (held in 1971)

George C. Scott didn't believe in acting competitions, so when he was nominated as Best Supporting Actor for *The Hustler* (1961) he asked the Academy to withdraw his nomination (the Academy declined his request, and Scott didn't win the Oscar). When Scott was nominated nine years later as Best Actor for *Patton* (1970), he repeated his request, but again the Academy declined, pointing out that it was Scott's performance, not Scott himself, that was being nominated. His name stayed on the ballot, and this time Scott won. Scott didn't attend the ceremony, and when his Oscar was later delivered to him he returned it to the Academy. Two years later Marlon Brando refused his Best Actor Oscar with a show-stopping announcement that's discussed in the list called "The Oddfather: 25 Awkward Moments at the Academy Awards Ceremony."

- Best Actor: George C. Scott, *Patton* (1970)

11. Forty-fifth ceremony (held in 1973)

The Godfather (1972) had ten Oscar nominations, but it actually started with eleven, which would have made it *il capo di tutti capi* with the most nominations for any movie that year. Originally, composer Nino Rota was nominated for his music score, but prior to the ceremony the Academy discovered that some of his music derived from his earlier score for the non-nominated Italian movie *Fortunella* (1958), and so Rota's nomination was withdrawn. *Sleuth* (1972) gained the vacant slot among the five nominated movies. The winner in this category was itself controversial, since the Oscar went to *Limelight* (1952). The Academy's rules require movies to play for a week in Los Angeles in order to be eligible for Oscars, but Charles Chaplin's twenty-year-old movie wasn't shown in an L.A. theater until 1972, making it the record-holder for the movie with the longest gap between its initial release and its Oscar win.

- Best Music (Original Dramatic Score): Charles Chaplin, Ray Rasch, and Larry Russell, *Limelight* (1952)

12. Fifty-seventh ceremony (held in 1985)

One of the nominees at this ceremony was P.H. Vazak, who, according to the movie's credits, wrote *Greystoke: The Legend of Tarzan, Lord of the Apes* (1984). Vazak was actually Robert Towne, who was unhappy with the finished film and so wrote under a pseudonym that turned out to be the name of his dog. Who knows what kind of acceptance speech there would have been had the dog won.

- Best Writing (Screenplay Based on Material from Another Medium): Peter Shaffer, *Amadeus* (1984)

13. Sixty-fifth ceremony (held in 1993)

Nominated for Best Foreign Language Film, *A Place in the World* (1992) was removed from the ballot before anyone could vote for it.

The Academy decided that Uruguay, the country that had submitted *A Place in the World* for consideration, had "insufficient Uruguayan artistic control" for a movie made with a cast, crew, and locations that were mostly Argentinian. Thus four countries, not the usual five, were officially nominated in this category, with France's entry emerging as the winner.

- Best Foreign Language Film: *Indochine* (1992)

14. Seventy-fifth ceremony (held in 2003)

In a situation similar to the Robert Towne/P.H. Vazak nomination at the aforementioned fifty-seventh ceremony (held in 1985), eighteen years later the Academy nominated co-screenwriters Charlie Kaufman and his twin brother Donald Kaufman for their screenplay for *Adaptation.* (2002). Donald, however, was Charlie's fictional invention and didn't really exist. Audiences never got to see what would have happened at the podium had the Kaufmans won, because the Oscar went to someone else.

- Best Writing (Adapted Screenplay): Ronald Harwood, *The Pianist* (2002)

15. Eighty-fourth ceremony (held in 2012)

Tuba Atlantic (2010) was a Best Short Film (Live Action) nominee until the Academy learned that it had been shown on TV before it had played in theaters. Because of this rules violation, the Academy rescinded the nomination five months *after* the Oscar had already been presented to another movie.

- Best Short Film (Live Action): *The Shore* (2011)

16. Eighty-sixth ceremony (held in 2014)

The theme song for the movie *Alone Yet Not Alone* (2013) was announced as an Oscar nominee. Unfortunately, before the final vote one of the songwriters improperly promoted his song to Academy members, so the Academy took "Alone Yet Not Alone" off the ballot, leaving four nominees.

- Best Music (Original Song): *Frozen* (2012)

17. Ninety-fifth ceremony (held in 2023)

Andrea Riseborough's acclaimed performance as an alcoholic single mother in *To Leslie* (2022) brought her a nomination for Best Actress, and also some controversy. Her small, independent movie had not been widely released (it's said to have earned a meager $27,000 in its extremely limited run), and it didn't have the budget for a major P.R. campaign that would have pushed a nomination for Riseborough by getting her onto talk shows and magazine covers.

What *To Leslie* did have was a large group of famous advocates. Before nominations were announced in January 2023, Jennifer Aniston, Cate Blanchett, Jane Fonda, Helen Hunt, Edward Norton, Gwyneth Paltrow, Susan Sarandon, Kate Winslet and others publicly and passionately championed Riseborough at screenings and on social media.

People started to wonder if anyone associated with the movie had privately reached out to these prominent stars in hopes they'd endorse a nomination for Riseborough. The Academy prohibits aggressive promotion via personal contact to individual Academy members (as noted in the previous entry about the eighty-sixth ceremony), and indeed Academy leaders did meet to discuss the situation. Ultimately they decided not to retract her nomination, Riseborough attended the March ceremony, and during that night's telecast she was shown giving a standing ovation to the actress who claimed the Oscar in her category.

- Best Actress: Michelle Yeoh, *Everything Everywhere All at Once* (2022)

BEST PICTURE

8 Major Developments in the Best Picture Category

Traditionally the last award shown at the annual Oscars telecast is for the category we generally call Best Picture, and for decades it had five nominees per ceremony. But Best Picture wasn't always the name for this category, and five wasn't always the number of nominees, as shown below.

1. First ceremony (held in 1929)

For this first year, and *only* for this first year, there were two top awards, one called Outstanding Picture and the other called Unique and Artistic Picture. Each classification had three nominees, with the following two winners.

Wings (1927).

- Outstanding Picture: *Wings* (1927)
- Unique and Artistic Picture: *Sunrise* (1927)

2. Second ceremony (held in 1930)

At the second ceremony, the Unique and Artistic Picture category was dropped, leaving just one final award presented to one movie chosen from five nominees. About three-fourths of the subsequent ceremonies have had five Best Picture nominees.

- Outstanding Picture: *The Broadway Melody* (1929)

3. Third ceremony (held in 1930)

Continuing the streak of annual changes to its most prestigious category, the Academy renamed the Outstanding Picture award Outstanding Production. The number of nominees remained at five.

- Outstanding Production: *All Quiet on the Western Front* (1930)

4. Fifth ceremony (held in 1932)

The Academy continued to tinker with its top award, this time by increasing the number of nominees to as many as the voters deemed appropriate. From this fifth ceremony to the sixteenth, the ceremonies averaged ten nominees per year, reaching a high of twelve at the seventh and eighth ceremonies (held in 1935 and 1936).

- Outstanding Production: *Grand Hotel* (1932)

5. Fourteenth ceremony (held in 1942)

A new decade and a new name for the Outstanding Production category, which was now to be called Outstanding Motion Picture.

- Outstanding Motion Picture: *How Green Was My Valley* (1941)

6. Seventeenth ceremony (held in 1945)

"Best" was finally introduced to this category's name. In addition, the number of nominees settled back to five, where it would stay for the next sixty-four years.

- Best Motion Picture: *Going My Way* (1944)

7. Thirty-fifth ceremony (held in 1963)

The Best Motion Picture award got one more revision to the name still used today.

- Best Picture: *Lawrence of Arabia* (1962)

8. Eighty-second ceremony (held in 2010)

Hoping to attract a bigger audience by including a wider range of movies, the Academy expanded the number of Best Picture nominees, beginning with a jump from five to ten at the eighty-second ceremony. At subsequent ceremonies, the number of nominees shifted from eight to nine to ten, finally settling on a fixed ten nominees at the ninety-fourth ceremony (held in 2022). In 2018 the Academy seriously considered another expansion that would have welcomed even more mass-market super-hero blockbusters into the proceedings; many of the Academy's revisions and decisions have been applauded, but the proposed Best Popular Movie category wasn't one of them, and the idea was soon rejected. The 2022 ceremony did include mentions of two "fan favorites," based on Twitter votes, but these movies were not official Oscar recipients.

- Best Picture: *The Hurt Locker* (2008)

95 Best Picture Winners and Their Additional Nominations

Now showing, every Best Picture winner from all ninety-five Academy Awards ceremonies. The movies are grouped by the number of overall nominations, including Best Picture. Then, movies within each group are listed by number of actual *wins*, from most to least.

It's interesting to note that the average number of Oscar nominations for a Best Picture winner rounds off to nine, and the average number of wins is five. As shown below, the three Best Picture winners that achieved those exact averages are three classics bunched together in the second half of the '70s: *One Flew Over the Cuckoo's Nest* (1975); *The Deer Hunter* (1978); and *Kramer vs. Kramer* (1979).

Incidentally, you might notice some of the Best Picture winners being used as subheads for our lists (you've already passed "Disquiet on the Western Front," "Gone with the Hour Hand," "The Greatest Shows on Earth," "Extraordinary People," and several others that wink at movies listed below). All part of the endless *Cavalcade* that is *The Academy Awards® Book of Lists*.

FOURTEEN NOMINATIONS

1. *Titanic* (1997): 11 wins
2. *All About Eve* (1950): 6

THIRTEEN NOMINATIONS

3. *From Here to Eternity* (1953): 8 wins
4. *Gone with the Wind* (1939): 8
5. *Shakespeare in Love* (1998): 7
6. *Chicago* (2002): 6
7. *Forrest Gump* (1994): 6
8. *The Shape of Water* (2017): 4

TWELVE NOMINATIONS

9. *Ben-Hur* (1959): 11 wins
10. *The English Patient* (1996): 9
11. *My Fair Lady* (1964): 8
12. *On the Waterfront* (1954): 8
13. *Dances with Wolves* (1990): 7
14. *Schindler's List* (1993): 7
15. *Mrs. Miniver* (1942): 6
16. *Gladiator* (2000): 5
17. *The King's Speech* (2010): 4

ELEVEN NOMINATIONS

18. *The Lord of the Rings: The Return of the King* (2003): 11 wins
19. *West Side Story* (1961): 10
20. *Amadeus* (1984): 8
21. *Gandhi* (1982): 8
22. *Everything Everywhere All at Once* (2022): 7
23. *Out of Africa* (1985): 7
24. *The Godfather: Part II* (1974): 6
25. *Oliver!* (1968): 5
26. *Terms of Endearment* (1983): 5
27. *The Godfather* (1972): 3
28. *Rebecca* (1940): 2

TEN NOMINATIONS

29. *Slumdog Millionaire* (2008): 8 wins
30. *Lawrence of Arabia* (1962): 7
31. *Patton* (1970): 7
32. *The Sting* (1973): 7
33. *The Apartment* (1960): 5
34. *The Artist* (2011): 5
35. *Braveheart* (1995): 5
36. *Going My Way* (1944): 5
37. *How Green Was My Valley* (1941): 5
38. *The Sound of Music* (1965): 5
39. *Tom Jones* (1963): 4
40. *The Life of Emile Zola* (1937): 3
41. *Rocky* (1976): 3

NINE NOMINATIONS

42. *Gigi* (1958): 9 wins
43. *The Last Emperor* (1987): 9
44. *The Hurt Locker* (2008): 6
45. *The Deer Hunter* (1978): 5
46. *Kramer vs. Kramer* (1979): 5
47. *One Flew Over the Cuckoo's Nest* (1975): 5
48. *Birdman or (The Unexpected Virtue of Ignorance)* (2014): 4
49. *Driving Miss Daisy* (1989): 4
50. *Unforgiven* (1992): 4
51. *12 Years a Slave* (2013): 3

EIGHT NOMINATIONS

52. *The Best Years of Our Lives* (1946): 7 wins

53. *The Bridge on the River Kwai* (1957): 7

54. *An American in Paris* (1951): 6

55. *A Man for All Seasons* (1966): 6

56. *American Beauty* (1999): 5

57. *Around the World in 80 Days* (1956): 5

58. *The French Connection* (1971): 5

59. *A Beautiful Mind* (2001): 4

60. *Marty* (1955): 4

61. *No Country for Old Men* (2007): 4

62. *Platoon* (1986): 4

63. *Rain Man* (1988): 4

***Rain Man* (1988).**

64. *Casablanca* (1942): 3

65. *Gentleman's Agreement* (1947): 3

66. *Moonlight* (2016): 3

67. *Mutiny on the Bounty* (1935): 1

SEVEN NOMINATIONS

68. *In the Heat of the Night* (1967): 5 wins

69. *The Silence of the Lambs* (1991): 5

70. *Chariots of Fire* (1981): 4

71. *Hamlet* (1948): 4

72. *The Lost Weekend* (1945): 4

73. *Million Dollar Baby* (2004): 4

74. *All the King's Men* (1949): 3

75. *Argo* (2012): 3

76. *Cimarron* (1931): 3

77. *The Great Ziegfeld* (1936): 3

78. *Midnight Cowboy* (1969): 3

79. *You Can't Take It with You* (1938): 2

SIX NOMINATIONS

80. *Ordinary People* (1980): 4 wins

81. *Parasite* (2019): 4

82. *Crash* (2004): 3

83. *Nomadland* (2020): 3

84. *Spotlight* (2015): 2

FIVE NOMINATIONS

85. *It Happened One Night* (1934): 5 wins

86. *Annie Hall* (1977): 4

87. *The Departed* (2006): 4

88. *Green Book* (2018): 3

89. *The Greatest Show on Earth* (1952): 2

FOUR NOMINATIONS

90. *Cavalcade* (1933): 3 wins
91. *All Quiet on the Western Front* (1930): 2

THREE NOMINATIONS

92. *CODA* (2021): 3 wins
93. *The Broadway Melody* (1929): 1

TWO NOMINATIONS

94. *Wings* (1927): 2 wins

ONE NOMINATION

95. *Grand Hotel* (1932): 1 win

8 Word-Counts in the Titles of All Ninety-Five Best Picture Winners

Want your movie to win the Academy Award for Best Picture? Keep the title short, because almost half of the Best Picture winners, including a recent streak of four in a row, have one- or two-word titles. Sample titles are given (the sample titles are the first and last movies to have that number of words in their titles).

1. Twenty-seven have one-word titles

- *Wings* (1927)
- *CODA* (2021)

2. Eighteen have two-word titles

- *Grand Hotel* (1932)
- *Green Book* (2018)

3. Twenty-four have three-word titles

- *The Broadway Melody* (1929)
- *The King's Speech* (2010)

4. Ten have four-word titles

- *It Happened One Night* (1934)
- *The Shape of Water* (2017)

5. Seven have five-word titles

- *The Life of Emile Zola* (1937)
- *Everything Everywhere All at Once* (2022)

6. Seven have six-word titles

- *All Quiet on the Western Front* (1930)
- *One Flew Over the Cuckoo's Nest* (1975)

7. One has a seven-word title

- *Birdman or (The Unexpected Virtue of Ignorance)* (2014)

8. One has a ten-word title

- *The Lord of the Rings: The Return of the King* (2003)

10 Pairs of Best Picture Nominees with the Same Titles

This list is limited to movies with the same titles that all got Best Picture nominations. Consequently, other pairs of movies with the same titles and Oscar nominations in various categories—such as *The Champ* (1931 and 1979), *Henry V* (1944 and 1989), *Imitation of Life* (1934 and 1959), *The Letter* (1929 and 1940), *The Patriot* (1928 and 2000), and *Titanic* (1953 and 1997)—aren't included, because in each pair only *one* of the movies was nominated for Best Picture. *Moulin Rouge* (1952) and *Moulin Rouge!* (2001) are rounded off as basically the same title, so they're shown in the following list. Got all that?

One more question on the side: can you name the only three Best Picture *winners* (including their years) among this list's bounty of Best Picture nominees?

1. *All Quiet on the Western Front* (1930 and 2022)
2. *Cleopatra* (1934 and 1963)
3. *Heaven Can Wait* (1943 and 1978)

4. *Les Misérables* (1935 and 2012)
5. *Little Women* (1933 and 2019)
6. *Moulin Rouge/Moulin Rouge!* (1952 and 2001)
7. *Mutiny on the Bounty* (1935 and 1962)
8. *A Star Is Born* (1937 and 2018)
9. *Romeo and Juliet* (1936 and 1968)
10. *West Side Story* (1961 and 2021)

Out of America: 42 Best Picture Winners Set Outside the United States

If you're trying to win the Oscar for Best Picture, your odds improve if you set your movie in the United States. That's often a cheaper option than setting your movie in a foreign country and then filming there. What's more, domestic settings appeal to Academy voters. Over half of the ninety-five Best Picture winners (fifty-two, or 55%) have told a story with a geographical location inside America's borders. Nine of the ten Best Picture winners made after 2012 have American settings, with *Parasite* (2019) the only exception.

Presented below are the forty-two Best Picture winners set beyond American borders. When a movie had both American and international settings, we went with the location that seemed the most vital to the story. Thus *The Deer Hunter* (1978), which has long, riveting acts set in Vietnam, appears on the following list, while *Forrest Gump* (1994), which has a Vietnam section but is mostly set in America, does not.

AFRICA

1. *Casablanca* (1942)
2. *The English Patient* (1996)
3. *Out of Africa* (1985)

ASIA/INDIA

4. *The Bridge on the River Kwai* (1957)
5. *The Deer Hunter* (1978)
6. *Gandhi* (1982)
7. *Platoon* (1986)
8. *The Last Emperor* (1987)
9. *Slumdog Millionaire* (2008)
10. *Parasite* (2019)

EUROPE

11. *Wings* (1927)
12. *All Quiet on the Western Front* (1930)
13. *Grand Hotel* (1932)
14. *Cavalcade* (1933)
15. *The Life of Emile Zola* (1937)
16. *Rebecca* (1940)
17. *How Green Was My Valley* (1941)
18. *Mrs. Miniver* (1942)
19. *Hamlet* (1948)
20. *An American in Paris* (1951)

21. *Gigi* (1958)
22. *Tom Jones* (1963)
23. *My Fair Lady* (1964)
24. *The Sound of Music* (1965)
25. *A Man for All Seasons* (1966)
26. *Oliver!* (1968)
27. *Patton* (1970)
28. *Chariots of Fire* (1981)
29. *Amadeus* (1984)
30. *Schindler's List* (1993)
31. *Braveheart* (1995)
32. *Shakespeare in Love* (1998)
33. *Gladiator* (2000)
34. *The King's Speech* (2010)

MIDDLE EAST

35. *Ben-Hur* (1959)
36. *Lawrence of Arabia* (1962)
37. *The Hurt Locker* (2008)
38. *Argo* (2012)

OCEANS

39. *Mutiny on the Bounty* (1935)
40. *Titanic* (1997)

VARIOUS/UNDEFINED INTERNATIONAL LOCATIONS

41. *Around the World in 80 Days* (1956)
42. *The Lord of the Rings: The Return of the King* (2003)

55 Best Picture Winners Set in the Past

What's nice about movies set in the past is that they usually don't date the way movies set in the present sometimes do, if only because the fashions, music, and attitudes of contemporary movies can quickly go out of style. Think of the Oscar-nominated *Saturday Night Fever* (1977), which was set in the "present day" (roughly the year the movie came out): back then, it was wildly popular and stylistically influential, but today it's more like one for the time capsule, at best a guilty pleasure (though a pleasure nonetheless). As a refresher, here are ten examples of "present day" Best Picture winners released in different decades: *It Happened One Night* (1934); *The Lost Weekend* (1945); *Marty* (1955); *Midnight Cowboy* (1969); *Rocky* (1976); *Rain Man* (1988); *The Silence of the Lambs* (1991); *Slumdog Millionaire* (2008); *Parasite* (2019); and *CODA* (2021).

Maybe being set in the past explains why so many Best Picture winners seem timeless. As shown in the following list, over half of them (fifty-five out of ninety-five, approximately 58%) have historical settings. You might've forgotten that some of these movies were set in earlier years, as with *The Shape of Water* (2017), which takes place in 1962, and *Nomadland* (2020), which starts in 2011.

Many of the movies span several decades—*The Great Ziegfeld* (1936) and *Forrest Gump* (1994), to name two—and with all the overlap it would've been impossible to list the movies in chronological order of their precise time settings. Thus we've grouped them together by century and then listed the individual movies in the chronological order of their release date. Interestingly, no movie set entirely in the future has ever won the Best Picture Oscar. In fact, very few futuristic movies have even been nominated, among them *A Clockwork Orange* (1971); *Avatar* (2009); *Her* (2013); and *Dune* (2021).

EARLY TWENTY-FIRST CENTURY
(IN YEARS BEFORE THE MOVIE'S RELEASE)

1. *Spotlight* (2015)
2. *Nomadland* (2020)

TWENTIETH CENTURY
(IN YEARS BEFORE THE MOVIE'S RELEASE)

3. *Wings* (1927)
4. *All Quiet on the Western Front* (1930)
5. *Cavalcade* (1933)
6. *The Great Ziegfeld* (1936)
7. *From Here to Eternity* (1953)
8. *The Bridge on the River Kwai* (1957)
9. *Lawrence of Arabia* (1962)
10. *My Fair Lady* (1964)
11. *The Sound of Music* (1965)

The Sound of Music (1965).

12. *Patton* (1970)
13. *The Godfather* (1972)

14. *The Sting* (1973)
15. *The Godfather: Part II* (1974)
16. *Out of Africa* (1985)
17. *The Deer Hunter* (1978)
18. *Chariots of Fire* (1981)
19. *Gandhi* (1982)
20. *Platoon* (1986)
21. *The Last Emperor* (1987)
22. *Driving Miss Daisy* (1989)
23. *Schindler's List* (1993)
24. *Forrest Gump* (1994)
25. *The English Patient* (1996)
26. *Titanic* (1997)
27. *A Beautiful Mind* (2001)
28. *Chicago* (2002)
29. *No Country for Old Men* (2007)
30. *The King's Speech* (2010)
31. *The Artist* (2011)
32. *Argo* (2012)
33. *Moonlight* (2016)
34. *The Shape of Water* (2017)
35. *Green Book* (2018)

NINETEENTH CENTURY

36. *Cimarron* (1931)
37. *The Life of Emile Zola* (1937)
38. *Gone with the Wind* (1939)
39. *How Green Was My Valley* (1941)
40. *Around the World in 80 Days* (1956)
41. *Gigi* (1958)
42. *Oliver!* (1968)
43. *Dances with Wolves* (1990)

44. *Unforgiven* (1992)
45. *12 Years a Slave* (2013)

EIGHTEENTH CENTURY

46. *Mutiny on the Bounty* (1935)
47. *Tom Jones* (1963)
48. *Amadeus* (1984)

THIRTEENTH-SIXTEENTH CENTURY

49. *Hamlet* (1948)
50. *A Man for All Seasons* (1966)
51. *Braveheart* (1995)

Braveheart (1995).

52. *Shakespeare in Love* (1998)

FIRST-SECOND CENTURY

53. *Ben-Hur* (1959)
54. *Gladiator* (2000)

DISTANT PAST

55. *The Lord of the Rings: The Return of the King* (2003)

21 Best Picture Winners Set in the United States and in the Past

Using the previous two lists of Best Picture winners, we can create a third list of movies that were almost destined for the top Oscar simply because of their settings. We already know that fifty-two of the ninety-five Best Picture winners were set in America, and fifty-five of the ninety-five were set in the past (those percentages are pretty close, 55% and 58%). If you create a Venn diagram of these two groups (each group inside a circle, the two circles side by side), then the overlapping section includes all the movies that belong to both groups. Listed below chronologically are those twenty-one movies that have both the geographical and temporal settings the Academy seemingly prefers in its Best Picture winners. As in other areas of life, it's location, location, location.

1. *Cimarron* (1931)
2. *The Great Ziegfeld* (1936)
3. *Gone with the Wind* (1939)
4. *From Here to Eternity* (1953)
5. *The Godfather* (1972)
6. *The Sting* (1973)
7. *The Godfather: Part II* (1974)
8. *Driving Miss Daisy* (1989)
9. *Dances with Wolves* (1990)
10. *Unforgiven* (1992)
11. *Forrest Gump* (1994)
12. *A Beautiful Mind* (2001)
13. *Chicago* (2002)
14. *No Country for Old Men* (2007)
15. *The Artist* (2011)
16. *12 Years a Slave* (2013)
17. *Spotlight* (2015)
18. *Moonlight* (2016)
19. *The Shape of Water* (2017)
20. *Green Book* (2018)
21. *Nomadland* (2020)

Mrs. Rebecca Miniver: 26 Best Picture Winners About a Leading Female Character

Whereas the previous lists show the importance of settings as you get ready to make your Best Picture-winning movie, this next list tells you who to make it about. In a word, men. Only 27% of the ninety-five Best Picture winners have been about a leading female character in the way that the movie shown below, *Out of Africa* (1985), is about Meryl Streep's character "Karen"—without her, there's no movie. Occasionally male characters have completely dominated a Best Picture winner to the total exclusion of all female characters, as in *Lawrence of Arabia* (1962) and *Patton* (1970), neither of which has a single speaking part for a woman; in contrast, there's no Best Picture counterpart with a 100% female cast.

In this next chronological list of twenty-six Best Picture winners that are about women, we've included movies that focused on a leading couple even if the male character was in the movie more, as with *Casablanca* (1942) and *The Apartment* (1960). Both of those classics have memorable female leads, so they're on the list. Note that there may be a trend in recent years towards actress-oriented Best Picture winners, but generally the movies shown below spread out pretty evenly across the decades. And remember, for every Best Picture-winning movie shown below that's mostly about women, there are *three* that are mostly about men.

1. *The Broadway Melody* (1929)
2. *It Happened One Night* (1934)
3. *Gone with the Wind* (1939)
4. *Rebecca* (1940)
5. *Mrs. Miniver* (1942)
6. *Casablanca* (1942)
7. *All About Eve* (1950)
8. *Gigi* (1958)
9. *The Apartment* (1960)
10. *West Side Story* (1961)
11. *My Fair Lady* (1964)
12. *The Sound of Music* (1965)
13. *One Flew Over the Cuckoo's Nest* (1975)
14. *Annie Hall* (1977)
15. *Terms of Endearment* (1983)
16. *Out of Africa* (1985)
17. *Driving Miss Daisy* (1989)
18. *The Silence of the Lambs* (1991)
19. *Titanic* (1997)

***Out of Africa* (1985).**

20. *Shakespeare in Love* (1998)
21. *Chicago* (2002)
22. *Million Dollar Baby* (2004)
23. *The Shape of Water* (2017)
24. *Nomadland* (2020)
25. *CODA* (2021)
26. *Everything Everywhere All at Once* (2022)

Die-tanic: 14 Best Picture Winners That Killed Off the Title Character

Starting with some of the earliest winners—*Wings* (1927) and *All Quiet on the Western Front* (1930)—and continuing through the decades—*The Bridge on the River Kwai* (1957) and *Titanic* (1997)—right up to modern times—*The Departed* (2006) and *No Country for Old Men* (2007)—Hollywood has killed off lead characters in almost a third of the movies it has anointed as Best Picture. *Midnight Cowboy* (1969), *Terms of Endearment* (1983), and on and on—that's a lot of unhappy endings.

In fact, (spoiler alert!) fourteen times the *title* character died, sometimes not even making it to the last reel: "Rebecca" was never alive in *Rebecca* (1940), and Marlon Brando's character "Don Corleone" keeled over from a heart attack with twenty-five minutes left of *The Godfather* (1972). In this next list of the fourteen Best Picture winners that let their title characters expire, we've included *One Flew Over the Cuckoo's Nest* (1975), since in the last scene the title's "One"—Jack Nicholson ("Randle McMurphy")—dies in bed, and not in the good way.

1. *The Great Ziegfeld* (1936)
2. *The Life of Emile Zola* (1937)

3. *Rebecca* (1940)
4. *Hamlet* (1948)
5. *Lawrence of Arabia* (1962)
6. *A Man for All Seasons* (1966)
7. *The Godfather* (1972)
8. *One Flew Over the Cuckoo's Nest* (1975)
9. *Gandhi* (1982)
10. *Amadeus* (1984)
11. *Braveheart* (1995)
12. *The English Patient* (1996)
13. *Gladiator* (2000)
14. *Million Dollar Baby* (2004)

10 Longest and 10 Shortest Best Picture Winners

This list of twenty movies covers about a fifth of all the Best Picture winners. Between the extreme lengths of the ten longest and the ten shortest movies are seventy-five more that are closer in length to the average length for all ninety-five Best Picture winners. That average is 138 minutes, which is the exact length of *All About Eve* (1950), the only Best Picture winner to land on that precise mark. Interestingly, the ten shortest Best Picture winners were released, on average, in 1963. Meanwhile the ten longest winners were released, on average, in 1974. Good movies, it seems, have gotten longer over the decades. And note how short *short* really is: *Marty* (1955), a sweet movie with its heart in the right place, zips by in only an hour and a half, so you could watch it *twice* before you've watched any of the ten longest movies *once*.

Throughout the list, the time for each movie refers to its original release, not the length of a later special or restored edition that added or subtracted minutes. The original *Lawrence of Arabia* (1962), for instance, lost thirty-five minutes of scenes in later re-releases. Additionally, the lengths are for the movies themselves without any additional introductory musical overtures, intermissions, *entr'acte* music, and concluding "exit music." All of these extra features would add about seventeen minutes to *Gone with the Wind* (1939) if they were included.

TEN LONGEST BEST PICTURE WINNERS (LONGEST FIRST)

222 MINUTES

1. *Lawrence of Arabia* (1962)

221 MINUTES

2. *Gone with the Wind* (1939)

212 MINUTES

3. *Ben-Hur* (1959)

201 MINUTES

4. *The Godfather: Part II* (1974)
5. *The Lord of the Rings: The Return of the King* (2003)

195 MINUTES

6. *Schindler's List* (1993)
7. *Titanic* (1997)

191 MINUTES

8. *Gandhi* (1982)

184 MINUTES

9. *The Deer Hunter* (1978)

182 MINUTES

10. *Around the World in 80 Days* (1956)

TEN SHORTEST BEST PICTURE WINNERS (SHORTEST FIRST)

NINETY MINUTES

1. *Marty* (1955)

NINETY-THREE MINUTES

2. *Annie Hall* (1977)

NINETY-NINE MINUTES

3. *Driving Miss Daisy* (1989)
4. *The Lost Weekend* (1945)

100 MINUTES

5. *The Artist* (2011)
6. *The Broadway Melody* (1929)

102 MINUTES

7. *Casablanca* (1942)

104 MINUTES

8. *The French Connection* (1971)

105 MINUTES

9. *It Happened One Night* (1934)
10. *Kramer vs. Kramer* (1979)

12 Streaks of Best Picture Winners in Black-and-White and in Color

The Oscar ceremony started with black-and-white movies and later embraced color movies. *Gone with the Wind* (1939) was the one that broke through. Producer David O. Selznick decided he had to roll the dice on what he hoped would be, at the time, the most magnificent Best Picture winner ever made. He did; it was; history.

However, the transition from black-to-white to color among Best Picture winners wasn't smooth, and it wasn't lasting. Below are the winning streaks of black-and-white and color movies in the Best Picture category, with the movies at the start and end of each streak listed.

1. First ceremony (held in 1929) to eleventh ceremony (held in 1939)

The first eleven Best Picture winners were in black and white.

- *Wings* (1927)
- *You Can't Take It with You* (1938)

2. Twelfth ceremony (held in 1940)

For the first time, a color movie won Best Picture, but this streak lasted only one year.

- *Gone with the Wind* (1939)

3. Thirteenth ceremony (held in 1941) to twenty-third ceremony (held in 1951)

A decade of black-and-white winners.

- *Rebecca* (1940)
- *All About Eve* (1950)

4. Twenty-fourth ceremony (held in 1952) to twenty-fifth ceremony (held in 1953)

Two years of Best Picture winners shot in color.

- *An American in Paris* (1951)
- *The Greatest Show on Earth* (1952)

5. Twenty-sixth ceremony (held in 1954) to twenty-eighth ceremony (held in 1956)

For three years, black-and-white winners went back to back to back.

- *From Here to Eternity* (1953)
- *Marty* (1955)

6. Twenty-ninth ceremony (held in 1957) to thirty-second ceremony (held in 1960)

Color triumphed for the next four years.

- *Around the World in 80 Days* (1956)
- *Ben-Hur* (1959)

7. Thirty-third ceremony (held in 1961)

We interrupt what would have been a long streak of color movies to bring you a single black-and-white winner.

- *The Apartment* (1960)

8. Thirty-fourth ceremony (held in 1962) to sixty-fifth ceremony (held in 1993)

Three straight decades of color winners.

- *West Side Story* (1961)
- *Unforgiven* (1992)

9. Sixty-sixth ceremony (held in 1994)

While Spielberg's 1993 masterpiece has moments of color, it's primarily in black and white.

- *Schindler's List* (1993)

10. Sixty-seventh ceremony (held in 1995) to eighty-third ceremony (held in 2011)

After a year with a black-and-white winner, for the next seventeen years color reigned in the Best Picture category.

- *Forrest Gump* (1994)
- *The King's Speech* (2010)

11. Eighty-fourth ceremony (held in 2012)

One last black-and-white movie before a new streak of color winners.

- *The Artist* (2011)

12. Eighty-fifth ceremony (held in 2013) to ninety-fifth ceremony (held in 2023)

The color juggernaut continues.

- *Argo* (2012)
- *Everything Everywhere All at Once* (2022)

11 Best Picture Winners That Were Followed by Sequels

If there's something Hollywood likes better than a great new idea, it's a great proven formula that will generate a *Part Two*, an *Episode III*, or a *Return of.* Consequently, eleven Best Picture-winning movies have generated sequels. The list below includes only the first sequel to each Best Picture winner, since a third movie would have been a sequel to the second, a fourth would have been a sequel to the third, and so on. The *Rocky* franchise, for instance, sprawls across eight movies—the first one awesome, some others so bad they're bad— but we're presenting just the original and its earliest sequel.

Discriminating viewers have long suffered from sequelphobia—a fear of bad sequels—and for good reason. Sequels might make money, but they rarely make history: see *Jaws 2* (1978) for a famous example of how quickly the original movie's Oscar-winning magic can disappear. *Caddyshack* (1980) was a beloved comedy classic; *Caddyshack II* (1988), not so much, proving again that just because a studio *can* make sequels doesn't mean it always *should* make sequels. The only Best Picture-winning original to have a Best Picture-winning sequel is number seven, *The Godfather* (1972); *The Lord of the Rings: The Return of the King* (2003) was itself a Best Picture-winning sequel, but it wasn't followed by any other *The Lord of the Rings* movies, so it doesn't appear on this list.

1. ***The Broadway Melody*** (1929)
- *Broadway Melody of 1936* (1935)
2. ***The Great Ziegfeld*** (1936)
- *Ziegfeld Girl* (1941)
3. ***Mrs. Miniver*** (1942)
- *The Miniver Story* (1950)
4. ***Going My Way*** **(1944)**
- *The Bells of St. Mary's* (1945)
5. ***In the Heat of the Night*** **(1967)**
- *They Call Me Mister Tibbs!* (1970)
6. ***The French Connection*** **(1971)**
- *French Connection II* (1975)

7. ***The Godfather* (1972)**
- *The Godfather: Part II* (1974)
8. ***The Sting* (1973)**
- *The Sting II* (1983)
9. ***Rocky* (1976)**
- *Rocky II* (1979)
10. ***Terms of Endearment* (1983)**
- *The Evening Star* (1996)
11. ***The Silence of the Lambs* (1991)**
- *Hannibal* (2001)

2 Trilogies with Every Movie in the Series Nominated for Best Picture

Two movie trilogies have had *every movie in the series* get a Best Picture nomination. That's a remarkable achievement, considering all the prominent trilogies that got just one, or not even one, Best Picture nomination for any entry in the series. To name four examples with zero Best Picture nominations anywhere in the trilogy: the first three movies that began with *Alien* (1979); with *Back to the Future* (1985); with *Jurassic Park* (1993); and with *The Dark Knight* (2008). Conversely, here are the two trilogies that earned Best Picture nominations for all three entries in the series, with winners indicated.

1. Three nominees, two wins for Best Picture

- **Winner** *The Godfather* (1972)
- **Winner** *The Godfather: Part II* (1974)
- *The Godfather: Part III* (1990)

2. Three nominees, one win for Best Picture

- *The Lord of the Rings: The Fellowship of the Ring* (2001)
- *The Lord of the Rings: The Two Towers* (2002)
- **Winner** *The Lord of the Rings: The Return of the King* (2003)

12 Months of Release Dates for Best Picture Winners

Best Picture-winning movies usually come out late in the year. At least, that's probably the general assumption. But is it true? To find out, we spread all of these winning movies' U.S. release dates across the calendar to produce the list shown below. Under each month is the Best Picture winner that was the latest release in that month.

Assign a number to each release date (January 1st = number one, December 31st = 365), add those numbers up, divide by ninety-five movies, and the average release date becomes day number 248. That's September 5th, exactly two-thirds of the way through the year. More importantly, the list clearly shows that Best Picture winners typically come out in the last quarter, proving that the general assumption is correct; in fact, approximately half of the ninety-five movies were released in October, November, or December. Even in the first decades of the Academy Awards ceremony, some of the Best Pictures were end-of-the-year releases: *Mutiny on the Bounty* (1935) premiered on November 8th, and *Gone with the Wind* (1939) on December 15th, to name two examples.

As you'll see from the following list, December is easily the most popular month for Best Picture winners, so maybe there is something to the theory that Academy voters tend to favor movies they've seen most recently as they choose winners early the next year. Interestingly, only one winner, *The Sting* (1973), came out exactly on Christmas Day.

1. January

- Three Best Picture winners
- *The Silence of the Lambs* (1991)

2. February

- Three Best Picture winners
- *It Happened One Night* (1934)

3. March

- Six Best Picture winners
- *Annie Hall* (1977)

4. April

- Five Best Picture winners
- *All Quiet on the Western Front* (1930)

5. May

- Six Best Picture winners
- *Midnight Cowboy* (1969)

6. June

- Four Best Picture winners
- *The Hurt Locker* (2008)

7. July

- One Best Picture winner
- *On the Waterfront* (1954)

8. August

- Eleven Best Picture winners
- *CODA* (2021)

9. September

- Nine Best Picture winners
- *Tom Jones* (1963)

10. October

- Ten Best Picture winners
- *How Green Was My Valley* (1941)

11. November

- Sixteen Best Picture winners
- *Schindler's List* (1993)

12. December

- Twenty-one Best Picture winners
- *Chicago* (2002)

3 Best Picture Winners Released in the "Wrong" Year

The familiar pattern of awarding the Best Picture Oscar to a movie that was released in the previous calendar year wasn't established until the seventh ceremony (held in 1935). Previously, one Best Picture winner—*Wings* (1927)—had come out *two years* before the 1929 ceremony when it won, and three other Best Picture winners—*All Quiet on the Western Front* (1930); *Cimarron* (1931); and *Grand Hotel* (1932)—had actually been released in the same year when the ceremony was held.

Starting with the 1935 ceremony that honored *It Happened One Night* and other 1934 movies, eighty-five of the next eighty-eight ceremonies named Best Picture winners that really were released in the previous calendar year. That leaves three exceptions when the winning movie came out in the "wrong" year, as explained below in chronological order.

1. *Casablanca* (1942) at the sixteenth ceremony (held in 1944)

- Scheduled for release in 1943, *Casablanca* was rushed into New York City theaters in November 1942 to capitalize on current World War Two events (especially the Allied invasion of North Africa and the naval battle at Casablanca's port) that were dominating that month's news.
- Academy rules state that a movie must play in a Los Angeles theater for at least one week to be eligible for Oscar consideration the following year; thus *Casablanca*, which opened in L.A. in January 1943, wasn't eligible for the awards presented at the fifteenth ceremony (held in 1943).

2. *Crash* (2004) at the seventy-eighth ceremony (held in 2006)

- Like *Casablanca* (1942), *Crash* got an early premiere (September 2004 at the Toronto International Film Festival), which explains its 2004 date.
- Because *Crash* wasn't released in L.A. until April 2005, it wasn't Oscar-eligible until the 2006 ceremony.

3. *The Hurt Locker* (2008) at the eighty-second ceremony (held in 2010)

- As with *Crash* (2004), *The Hurt Locker* was shown at international film festivals in 2008 and released domestically in 2009, making it eligible for the 2010 ceremony.
- Similarly, a later Best Picture nominee, *Sound of Metal* (2019), premiered at a 2019 film festival and then had a 2020 domestic release, making it eligible for the ninety-third ceremony (held in 2021).
- *Judas and the Black Messiah* (2021) actually came out in February of the same year as the April ceremony, but that 2021

ceremony had an extended eligibility period because of the COVID-19 pandemic, thus enabling *Judas* to qualify as a Best Picture nominee.

Screen Book: 36 Best Picture Winners Based on a Book with the Same Title

This next list could be called "Where They Came From, Part One." Each of the following Best Picture-winning movies shares a title with the full-length novel or nonfiction book it was based on.

A few of the titles below—*Rebecca* (1940), for example—detoured from the original books into adapted plays before Hollywood steered them onto the Oscar highway, but the movies derived more from the page than the stage (Best Picture-winning movies clearly based on famous plays or musicals are shown in the next list). We've "rounded off" some of the titles when they're close but not quite perfect matches: *Schindler's List* (1993), for instance, was based on the book *Schindler's Ark* by Thomas Keneally (1982), but it's still listed among the three-dozen movies listed below.

Movie Based on a Book (Year)	Author (Year the Book Was Published)
1. *All Quiet on the Western Front* (1930)	Erich Maria Remarque (1928)
2. *All the King's Men* (1949)	Robert Penn Warren (1946)
3. *Argo* (2012)	Antonio Mendez (2012)
4. *Around the World in 80 Days* (1956)	Jules Verne (1873)
5. *A Beautiful Mind* (2001)	Sylvia Nasar (1998)
6. *Ben-Hur* (1959)	Lew Wallace (1880)
7. *The Bridge on the River Kwai* (1957)	Pierre Boulle (1952)
8. *Cimarron* (1931)	Edna Ferber (1930)

9. *Dances with Wolves* (1990)	Michael Blake (1988)
10. *The English Patient* (1996)	Michael Ondaatje (1992)
11. *Forrest Gump* (1994)	Winston Groom (1986)
12. *The French Connection* (1971)	Robin Moore (1969)
13. *From Here to Eternity* (1953)	James Jones (1951)
14. *Gentleman's Agreement* (1947)	Laura Z. Hobson (1947)
15. *Gigi* (1958)	Colette (1944)
16. *The Godfather* (1972)	Mario Puzo (1969)
17. *The Godfather: Part II* (1974)	Mario Puzo (1969)
18. *Gone with the Wind* (1939)	Margaret Mitchell (1936)
19. *How Green Was My Valley* (1941)	Richard Llewellyn (1939)
20. *In the Heat of the Night* (1967)	John Ball (1965)
21. *Kramer vs. Kramer* (1979)	Avery Corman (1977)
22. *The Lord of the Rings: The Return of the King* (2003)	J.R.R. Tolkien (1955)
23. *The Lost Weekend* (1945)	Charles R. Jackson (1944)
24. *Midnight Cowboy* (1969)	James Leo Herlihy (1965)
25. *Mrs. Miniver* (1942)	Jan Struther (1940)
26. *Mutiny on the Bounty* (1935)	Charles Nordhoff and James Norman Hall (1932)
27. *No Country for Old Men* (2007)	Cormac McCarthy (2005)
28. *One Flew Over the Cuckoo's Nest* (1975)	Ken Kesey (1962)
29. *Ordinary People* (1980)	Judith Guest (1976)

30. *Out of Africa* (1985)	Isak Dinesen (1937)
31. *Rebecca* (1940)	Daphne du Maurier (1938)
32. *Schindler's List* (1993)	Thomas Keneally (1982)
33. *The Silence of the Lambs* (1991)	Thomas Harris (1988)
34. *Terms of Endearment* (1983)	Larry McMurtry (1975)
35. *Tom Jones* (1963)	Henry Fielding (1749)
36. *12 Years a Slave* (2013)	Solomon Northup (1853)

The Broadway Memory: 14 Best Picture Winners Based on a Stage Play or Musical

A sequel to the previous list, this next one—"Where They Came From, Part Two" (aka, "Son of Where They Came From")—presents movies that have the same titles as the earlier stage plays or musicals they're based on, except where noted.

A question might arise about *Oliver!* (1968), since its origins are in *Oliver Twist*, Charles Dickens' 1838 novel, but the movie was actually based on *Oliver!*, Lionel Bart's 1960 stage musical. Ironically, the one Best Picture winner that actually has Broadway in its title—*The Broadway Melody* (1929)—was MGM's original creation and wasn't taken from a pre-existing musical.

Movie Based on a Play (Year)	**Play Title (If Different), Playwright (Year First Performed)**
1. *Amadeus* (1984)	Peter Shaffer (1979)
2. *Casablanca* (1942)	*Everybody Comes to Rick's*, Murray Burnett and Joan Alison (unproduced)
3. *Cavalcade* (1933)	Noël Coward (1931)
4. *Driving Miss Daisy* (1989)	Alfred Uhry (1987)

5. *Grand Hotel* (1932)	Edward Knoblock (1931)
6. *Hamlet* (1948)	William Shakespeare (early seventeenth century)
7. *A Man for All Seasons* (1966)	Robert Bolt (1960)
8. *Moonlight* (2016)	*In Moonlight Black Boys Look Blue*, Tarell Alvin McCraney (unpublished)
9. *You Can't Take It with You* (1938)	George S. Kaufman and Moss Hart (1936)
Movie Based on a Musical (Year)	**Creators of the Original Musical (Year First Performed)**
1. *Chicago* (2002)	John Kander, Fred Ebb, and Bob Fosse (1975)
2. *My Fair Lady* (1964)	Alan Jay Lerner and Frederick Loewe (1956)
3. *Oliver!* (1968)	Lionel Bart (1960)
4. *The Sound of Music* (1965)	Richard Rodgers, Oscar Hammerstein II, Howard Lindsay, and Russel Crouse (1959)
5. *West Side Story* (1961)	Leonard Bernstein, Stephen Sondheim, and Arthur Laurents (1957)

7 Major Studios Ranked by Best Picture Winners

Seven Hollywood studios—commonly known as Columbia, Fox, MGM, Paramount, United Artists, Universal, and Warner Bros.—have made seventy-six, or over four-fifths, of the ninety-five Best Picture-winning movies. In the following list, we've combined all the iterations of these companies into their short-hand names; thus, Twentieth-Century Fox Film Corps., 20th Century Fox (sans hyphen as of 1985), Twentieth Century Studios, and the subsidiary Fox Searchlight all come under the heading for Fox (which was the company's name when it won its first Best Picture Oscar). Similarly, Paramount represents the early twentieth century companies

Famous Players Film Co., Famous Players-Lasky, and Paramount Famous Lasky, which were all rolled under the name Paramount Pictures with a later subsidiary called Paramount Players.

You might be surprised to see which studio leads in Best Picture winners, since Metro-Goldwyn-Mayer (MGM) has had the durable reputation of being Hollywood's biggest and most successful studio. Indeed MGM won four of the first nine and six of the first fifteen Best Picture Oscars, but all of its Best Picture winners came out before 1960. After its *Ben-Hur* (1959) triumph, MGM never won another Oscar for Best Picture, and Fox (in various forms) sprinted by to become the new Best Picture leader. Surprisingly Disney, another famous studio, never made a Best Picture winner. But the seven leading studios did, and they're shown below with their first and last winners.

THIRTEEN WINS

1. Fox

- *Cavalcade* (1933)
- *Nomadland* (2020)

TWELVE WINS

2. Columbia

- *It Happened One Night* (1934)
- *The Last Emperor* (1987)

3. United Artists

- *Rebecca* (1940)
- *Rain Man* (1988)

ELEVEN WINS

4. Paramount

- *Wings* (1927)
- *Titanic* (1997)

TEN WINS

5. Warner Bros.

- *The Life of Emile Zola* (1937)

- *Argo* (2012)

NINE WINS

6. MGM

- *The Broadway Melody* (1929)
- *Ben-Hur* (1959)

7. Universal

- *All Quiet on the Western Front* (1930)
- *Green Book* (2018)

Argo for It: 10 Famous People Who Co-Produced Best Picture-Nominated Movies

At the first twenty-three Oscar ceremonies, the Academy presented its Best Picture award to studios and production companies, not to specific producers identified by name. Consequently, in those early years some famous people were behind the scenes producing Best Picture-nominated movies, but they weren't officially identified as potential Oscar recipients. Howard Hughes, for example, was already a famous millionaire and on his way to becoming one of the world's richest men, when he produced one of the Best Picture nominees—*The Racket* (1928)—at the very first Academy Awards ceremony. Hughes himself, though, wasn't listed as a nominee (his company, Caddo, was listed instead).

The Academy started identifying individual producers of the Best Picture nominees at the twenty-fourth ceremony (held in 1952). From then on, many prominent co-producers would be named as potential co-recipients of the Best Picture Oscar. Frequently these co-producers also directed the movies, a double assignment taken on multiple times by such legendary directors as Francis Ford Coppola, Clint Eastwood, Stanley Kubrick, Martin Scorsese, Steven Spielberg, and Robert Wise. Same thing with actors and actresses who produced the Best Picture-nominated movies they also starred in: Warren Beatty, Kevin Costner, Robert De Niro, Clint Eastwood, Henry Fonda, Frances McDormand, Will Smith, Barbra Streisand, Denzel Washington, and John Wayne are ten of the many stars who did double duty.

In addition to these famous names are ten more you'll recognize in the following list. What makes this next group unique is that all of them were nominated as the co-producer of a movie that was up for Best Picture, but they neither directed it nor had leading roles in it (small roles, possibly, but leading roles, no). They're listed below alphabetically along with a Best Picture-nominated movie each one produced (winning movies are marked **Winner**).

1. George Clooney

- **Winner** *Argo* (2012)

2. Bradley Cooper

- *Joker* (2019)

3. Matt Damon

- *Manchester by the Sea* (2016)

4. Danny DeVito

- *Erin Brockovich* (2000)

5. Michael Douglas

- **Winner** *One Flew Over the Cuckoo's Nest* (1975)

6. Quincy Jones

- *The Color Purple* (1985)

7. Frances McDormand

- *Women Talking* (2022)

8. Brad Pitt

- **Winner** *12 Years a Slave* (2013)

9. Pharrell Williams

- *Hidden Figures* (2016)

10. Oprah Winfrey

- *Selma* (2014)

MGM Grand: 1 Movie That Was Nominated for a Single Oscar—Best Picture—and Won

The category known today simply as Best Picture was called Outstanding Picture, Outstanding Production, Outstanding Motion Picture, and Best Motion Picture before the Academy settled on the current name at the thirty-fifth Academy Awards ceremony (held in 1963).

No matter what this category was called, only one time, in all the years dating back to the first ceremony (held in 1929), has a movie won this grand award without receiving any other nominations. That singular occurrence came when the category was still going by its original name. MGM's winning movie was wildly popular and, as the first major drama with an all-star cast, extremely influential (many subsequent epics with all-star casts were probably more entertaining in the initial pitch meeting than they were later in the theater, but this first one is still considered by many to be a timeless masterpiece). It's also the movie in which Greta Garbo speaks her famous "I want to be alone" line.

1. Outstanding Production: *Grand Hotel* (1932)

7 Best Picture Winners That Won Every Category They Were Nominated For

In ninety-five years of Academy Awards, only seven movies batted 1.000 by winning the Best Picture Oscar and then sweeping every remaining competitive category in which they were nominated. Those seven movies are listed below from the highest number of wins to the lowest.

Just missing the cut are another seven Best Picture winners that won every category they were nominated for except one: *Ben-Hur* (1959), eleven wins out of twelve nominations; *West Side Story* (1961), ten out of eleven; *The Best Years of Our Lives* (1946) and *The Bridge on the River Kwai* (1957), seven out of eight; *Annie Hall* (1977) and *The Departed* (2006), four out of five; and *Cavalcade*

(1933), three out of four. Remarkable, but not perfection, and perfection is what this next list celebrates.

ELEVEN WINS OUT OF ELEVEN NOMINATIONS

1. *The Lord of the Rings: The Return of the King* (2003)

NINE OUT OF NINE

2. *Gigi* (1958)
3. *The Last Emperor* (1987)

The Last Emperor (1987).

FIVE OUT OF FIVE

4. *It Happened One Night* (1934)

THREE OUT OF THREE

5. *CODA* (2021)

TWO OUT OF TWO

6. *Wings* (1927)

ONE OUT OF ONE

7. *Grand Hotel* (1932)

25 Best Picture Winners That Won the Fewest Oscars

The twenty-five chronologically listed Best Picture-winning movies shown below ended the Academy Awards ceremony with a total of three or fewer Oscars. Interestingly, over two-thirds (seventeen out of the twenty-five) came out before 1974, which is the halfway point in Academy Awards history, suggesting that the Academy was more likely to spread around its awards in its earlier decades.

But there's also another reason why Best Picture winners back in the day often won fewer Oscars than today's Best Picture winners typically win. In the ceremony's early years there were far fewer Oscar categories than there are now. As an example, *The Broadway Melody* (1929), shown below with just one win, competed in a year when there were only seven categories, whereas *Green Book* (2018), shown with three wins, competed when there were *twenty-four* categories and thus far more chances to win multiple Oscars. Still, if your movie is going to win only one, two, or three Oscars, Best Picture is definitely among the ones you want.

WON THREE OSCARS

1. *Cimarron* (1931)
2. *Cavalcade* (1933)
3. *The Great Ziegfeld* (1936)
4. *The Life of Emile Zola* (1937)
5. *Casablanca* (1942)
6. *Gentleman's Agreement* (1947)
7. *All the King's Men* (1949)
8. *Midnight Cowboy* (1969)
9. *The Godfather* (1972)
10. *Rocky* (1976)
11. *Crash* (2004)
12. *Argo* (2012)
13. *12 Years a Slave* (2013)
14. *Moonlight* (2016)
15. *Green Book* (2018)
16. *CODA* (2021)

WON TWO OSCARS

17. *Wings* (1927)
18. *All Quiet on the Western Front* (1930)
19. *You Can't Take It with You* (1938)
20. *Rebecca* (1940)
21. *The Greatest Show on Earth* (1952)
22. *Spotlight* (2015)

WON ONE OSCAR

23. *The Broadway Melody* (1929)
24. *Grand Hotel* (1932)
25. *Mutiny on the Bounty* (1935)

17 Best Picture Nominees with No Additional Nominations

Of the 589 movies that have been nominated for Best Picture (589, as of the awards given to 2022 movies), typically these nominees have claimed multiple Oscar nominations because they excelled in several areas (directing, cinematography, editing, music, etc.). Indeed, it's that multi-faceted excellence that made them Best Picture nominees.

However, the following chronologically listed movies, all of them up for Best Picture, earned no other nominations. Think of that: seventeen Best Picture nominees, and not a single additional nomination anywhere for acting, or writing, or music, or art direction, or any other category. Basically the Academy couldn't define *why* these seventeen movies were Best Picture-worthy, it just sensed they were.

Maybe the era had something to do with this phenomenon, because every movie shown below was made before 1943. In the 1920s and '30s the number of Oscar categories was often less than ten or in the teens, whereas by the mid-1940s the number was in the mid-twenties, thus giving movies more opportunities to earn multiple nominations. In the list, the only movie to win its sole nomination for Best Picture is marked **Winner**.

1. *The Racket* (1928)
2. *The Hollywood Revue of 1929* (1929)
3. *East Lynne* (1931)

4. *Five Star Final* (1931)
5. *The Smiling Lieutenant* (1931)
6. *Trader Horn* (1931)
7. **Winner** *Grand Hotel* (1932)
8. *One Hour with You* (1932)
9. *Smilin' Through* (1932)
10. *She Done Him Wrong* (1933)
11. *Here Comes the Navy* (1934)
12. *The House of Rothschild* (1934)
13. *Ruggles of Red Gap* (1935)
14. *Libeled Lady* (1936)
15. *Grand Illusion* (1937)
16. *One Foot in Heaven* (1941)
17. *The Ox-Bow Incident* (1942)

14 Movies with at Least Eight Oscar Nominations (Including Best Picture) and Zero Wins

Somehow these fourteen movies were good enough to earn eight or more Oscar nominations, including one for Best Picture, but they weren't good enough to win even one award. Expanding this list by just one more nomination to seven or more would've added another nineteen movies, including some popular favorites like *Broadcast News* (1987); *Double Indemnity* (1944); *The Shawshank Redemption* (1994); and *The Fabelmans* (2022).

Even if the two co-leaders shown below hold a slightly embarrassing record, they're still soaring in rarified air with that many nominations, and rarified air is far better than no air at all. Do look at number eight, *Peyton Place* (1957) standing tall with nine nominations, even though for many viewers this long soap opera is more like a test that evaluates how much melodrama human beings can take (a lot, evidently, since the movie was a smash hit and spun off a popular TV series). For the following movies, we're counting only competitive Oscars, not any Honorary or Special Achievement awards.

ELEVEN NOMINATIONS

1. *The Color Purple* (1985)
2. *The Turning Point* (1977)

TEN NOMINATIONS

3. *American Hustle* (2013)
4. *Gangs of New York* (2002)
5. *The Irishman* (2019)
6. *True Grit* (2010)

NINE NOMINATIONS

7. *The Little Foxes* (1941)
8. *Peyton Place* (1957)
9. *The Banshees of Inisherin* (2022)

EIGHT NOMINATIONS

10. *The Elephant Man* (1980)
11. *The Nun's Story* (1959)
12. *Quo Vadis* (1951)
13. *The Remains of the Day* (1993)
14. *The Sand Pebbles* (1966)

6 Movies with at Least Eight Oscar Nominations But Not One for Best Picture

A half-dozen movies representing forty-nine Oscar nominations, with not a single nomination for Best Picture to be found anywhere. As in the previous list, opening up the list to seven or more nominations would've more than doubled the length with an additional thirteen movies, including *Aliens* (1986) and *Bullets Over Broadway* (1994).

Some of the great movies shown below did win multiple Oscars—*Dreamgirls* (2006) won two, for example. But somehow none of the six, though excellent in at least eight areas, made it into the pantheon of Best Picture nominees. Even without that ultimate recognition, a few of these movies made profound and lasting impressions: some enraptured viewers are still thinking up adjectives for *Close Encounters* and *The Dark Knight*, words like amazing, astonishing, astounding, awe-inspiring . . . and those are just the A's.

NINE NOMINATIONS

1. *They Shoot Horses, Don't They?* (1969)

EIGHT NOMINATIONS

2. *Close Encounters of the Third Kind* (1977)
3. *The Dark Knight* (2008)
4. *Dreamgirls* (2006)
5. *The Poseidon Adventure* (1972)
6. *Ragtime* (1981)

36 Times When the Movie with the Most Nominations *Didn't* Win for Best Picture

Upset Alert, Part One. In most years, the movie that has the most (or is tied for the most) Oscar nominations also wins the Oscar for Best Picture. But that didn't happen at thirty-six of the ninety-five ceremonies (over one-third of the time). Consider number thirty-one in the following list, when *three* Best Picture nominees—*High Noon* (1952); *Moulin Rouge* (1952); and *The Quiet Man* (1952)—were up for seven Oscars, yet there was *The Greatest Show on Earth* (1952) with only five nominations, standing on the shore and successfully waving its arms to flag down the Best Picture boat.

Listed in descending order from the most nominations on down, here are the upsets when the movies that were the leaders or co-leaders for the most nominations (the movies in **bold**) *didn't* win the Best Picture award. Sometimes the upset wasn't all that dramatic: *12 Years a Slave* (2013), which is shown below, technically qualifies as an upset winner, even though it had only one fewer nomination than that year's co-leaders. Underneath these movies are the ones that did win for Best Picture and their overall nominations.

FOURTEEN NOMINATIONS

1. *La La Land* (2016)
- *Moonlight* (2016), 8 nominations

THIRTEEN NOMINATIONS

2. *Mary Poppins* (1964)
- *My Fair Lady* (1964), 12 nominations

My Fair Lady (1964).

3. *The Curious Case of Benjamin Button* **(2008)**
- *Slumdog Millionaire* (2008), 10 nominations
4. *Who's Afraid of Virginia Woolf?* **(1966)**
- *A Man for All Seasons* (1966), 8 nominations
5. *The Lord of the Rings: The Fellowship of the Ring* **(2001)**
- *A Beautiful Mind* (2001), 8 nominations

TWELVE NOMINATIONS

6. *The Song of Bernadette* **(1943)**
- *Casablanca* (1942), 8 nominations
7. *A Streetcar Named Desire* **(1951)**
- *An American in Paris* (1951), 8 nominations
8. *Johnny Belinda* **(1948)**
- *Hamlet* (1948), 7 nominations
9. *Reds* **(1981)**
- *Chariots of Fire* (1981), 7 nominations
10. *Lincoln* **(2012)**
- *Argo* (2012), 7 nominations
11. *The Revenant* **(2015)**
- *Spotlight* (2015), 6 nominations
12. *The Power of the Dog* **(2021)**
- *CODA* (2021), 3 nominations

ELEVEN NOMINATIONS

13. *Sergeant York* **(1941)**
- *How Green Was My Valley* (1941), 10 nominations
14. *Hugo* **(2011)**
- *The Artist* (2011), 10 nominations
15. *The Aviator* **(2004)**
- *Million Dollar Baby* (2004), 7 nominations

16. *Joker* **(2019)**

- *Parasite* (2019), 6 nominations

17. *Julia* **(1977) and** *The Turning Point* **(1977)**

- *Annie Hall* (1977), 5 nominations

TEN NOMINATIONS

18. *American Hustle* **(2013) and** *Gravity* **(2013)**

- *12 Years a Slave* (2013), 9 nominations

12 Years a Slave (2013).

19. *Giant* **(1956)**

- *Around the World in 80 Days* (1956), 8 nominations

20. *Sayonara* **(1957)**

- *The Bridge on the River Kwai* (1957), 8 nominations

21. *Bonnie and Clyde* **(1967) and** *Guess Who's Coming to Dinner* **(1967)**

- *In the Heat of the Night* (1967), 7 nominations

22. *Anne of the Thousand Days* (1969)
- *Midnight Cowboy* (1969), 7 nominations

23. *Bugsy* (1991)
- *The Silence of the Lambs* (1991), 7 nominations

24. *Mank* (2020)
- *Nomadland* (2020), 6 nominations

25. *The Favourite* (2018) and *Roma* (2018)
- *Green Book* (2018), 5 nominations

EIGHT NOMINATIONS

26. *The Bells of St. Mary's* (1945)
- *The Lost Weekend* (1945), 7 nominations

27. *The Heiress* (1949)
- *All the King's Men* (1949), 7 nominations

28. *Raging Bull* (1980)
- *Ordinary People* (1980), 6 nominations

29. *Brokeback Mountain* (2005)
- *Crash* (2004), 6 nominations

30. *Dreamgirls* (2006)
- *The Departed* (2006), 5 nominations

SEVEN NOMINATIONS

31. *High Noon* (1952); *Moulin Rouge* (1952); and *The Quiet Man* (1952)
- *The Greatest Show on Earth* (1952), 5 nominations

SIX NOMINATIONS

32. *One Night of Love* (1934)
- *It Happened One Night* (1934), 5 nominations

33. *The Love Parade* (1929)
- *All Quiet on the Western Front* (1930), 4 nominations

FIVE NOMINATIONS

34. *In Old Arizona* (1928) and *The Patriot* (1928)
- *The Broadway Melody* (1929), 3 nominations

35. *7th Heaven* (1927)
- *Wings* (1927), 2 nominations

FOUR NOMINATIONS

36. *Arrowsmith* (1931) and *The Champ* (1931)
- *Grand Hotel* (1932), 1 nomination

20 Times When the Movie That Won the Most Oscars *Didn't* Win for Best Picture

Upset Alert, Part Two (aka, Son of Upset Alert). The previous list shows movies with the most nominations that didn't win the Best Picture Oscar. The next list shows movies that actually won the most Oscars that year yet still didn't win the top award. That's what happened at twenty of the ninety-five ceremonies (about one-fifth of the time). Those twenty upsets lead off with the movies (in **bold**) with the most Oscars, followed by the actual Best Picture winners and their overall wins.

As you'll see, the ceremony with the biggest disparity between the movie with the most wins and the year's Best Picture was the forty-fifth (held in 1973), shown at number one; that year, there was a five-win difference between *Cabaret*, which claimed eight Oscars, and the year's Best Picture, *The Godfather*, which won three.

EIGHT WINS

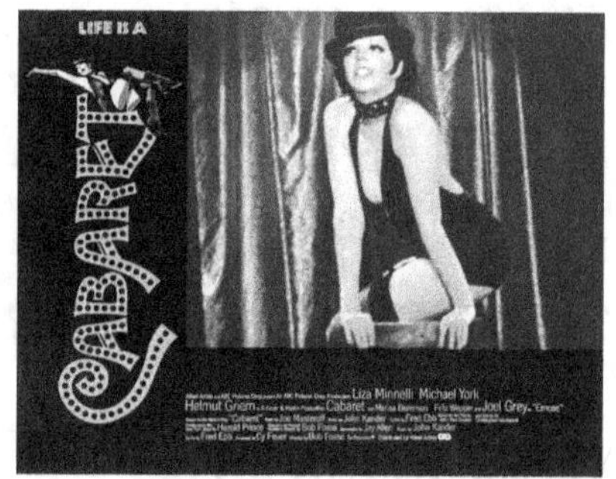

1. *Cabaret* **(1972)**
- *The Godfather* (1972), 3 wins

SEVEN WINS

2. *Gravity* **(2013)**
- *12 Years a Slave* (2013), 3 wins

SIX WINS

3. *Star Wars: Episode IV—A New Hope* **(1977)**
- *Annie Hall* (1977), 4 wins
4. *La La Land* **(2016)**
- *Moonlight* (2016), 3 wins
5. *Dune* **(2021)**
- *CODA* (2021), 3 wins
6. *Mad Max: Fury Road* **(2015)**
- *Spotlight* (2015), 2 wins

FIVE WINS

7. *The Aviator* **(2004)**
- *Million Dollar Baby* (2004), 4 wins

8. ***The Bad and the Beautiful* (1952)**
- *The Greatest Show on Earth* (1952), 2 wins

FOUR WINS

9. ***Anthony Adverse* (1936)**
- *The Great Ziegfeld* (1936), 3 wins
10. ***The Song of Bernadette* (1943)**
- *Casablanca* (1942), 3 wins
11. ***The Heiress* (1949)**
- *All the King's Men* (1949), 3 wins
12. ***Butch Cassidy and the Sundance Kid* (1969)**
- *Midnight Cowboy* (1969), 3 wins
13. ***All the President's Men* (1976) and *Network* (1976)**
- *Rocky* (1976), 3 wins
14. ***Life of Pi* (2012)**
- *Argo* (2012), 3 wins
15. ***Bohemian Rhapsody* (2018)**
- *Green Book* (2018), 3 wins
16. ***The Informer* (1935)**
- *Mutiny on the Bounty* (1935), 1 win

THREE WINS

17. ***7th Heaven* (1927) and *Sunrise* (1927)**
- *Wings* (1927), 2 wins
18. ***The Adventures of Robin Hood* (1938)**
- *You Can't Take It with You* (1938), 2 wins
19. ***The Thief of Bagdad* (1940)**
- *Rebecca* (1940), 2 wins

TWO WINS

20. *Bad Girl* (1931) and *The Champ* (1931)
- *Grand Hotel* (1932), 1 win

All About Peeve: 7 Movies with Valid Complaints That They Weren't Named Best Picture

Upset Alert, Part Three (aka, Revenge of the Upset Alert). Combining the previous two lists, this next one presents a summary of the seven movies that achieved two major landmarks when they were up for Academy Awards: they earned the year's most Oscar nominations *and* the year's most Oscar wins. Yet none of these elite movies was named the year's Best Picture, making them the seven movies that have valid complaints about not winning the top Oscar.

After adding up each movie's nominations and wins, we've put the seven movies (in **bold**) in descending order from the highest total to the lowest. The actual Best Picture winners and their totals follow. Look at number four, *The Song of Bernadette* (1943) clearly ahead but losing Best Picture to *Casablanca* (1942), a treasured movie most viewers don't just watch, they don't merely admire, they *love*. Ironically, *La La Land* (2016), the movie with the biggest legitimate gripe, was briefly named as Best Picture at the 2017 ceremony because the two presenters had been given the wrong envelope to open, a mistake quickly resolved in favor of *Moonlight* (2016).

Movie (Year)	Nominations	Wins	Total
1. *La La Land* (2016)	14	6	**20**
• *Moonlight* (2016)	8	3	11
2. *Gravity* (2013)	10	7	**17**
• *12 Years a Slave* (2013)	9	3	12
3. *The Aviator* (2004)	11	5	**16**
• *Million Dollar Baby* (2004)	7	4	11

4. *The Song of Bernadette* (**1943**)	**12**	**4**	**16**
▪ *Casablanca* (1942)	8	3	11
5. *The Heiress* (**1949**)	**8**	**4**	**12**
▪ *All the King's Men* (1949)	7	3	10
6. *7th Heaven* (**1927**)	**5**	**3**	**8**
▪ *Wings* (1927)	2	2	4
7. *The Champ* (**1931**)	**4**	**2**	**6**
▪ *Grand Hotel* (1932)	1	1	2

22 Highest- and Lowest-Rated Best Picture-Winning Movies at IMDb.com

Every movie fan is familiar with IMDb.com. Established in the early 1990s, the authoritative Internet Movie Database (IMDb) provides an incredible amount of detailed information about seemingly every movie (actually, around 581,000) and TV show ever made. One interesting aspect of the site is its fan-based rating system. Votes from eighty-three million registered users are tabulated and run through a formula that produces a number on a ten-point scale. IMDb then ranks the top 250 movies, based on their ratings. As of 2022, the number-one movie was *The Shawshank Redemption* (1994), its 9.3/10 rating putting it ahead (in some cases far ahead) of every Best Picture-winning movie.

But how do Best Picture winners fare among IMDb voters? Below are the eleven highest- and eleven lowest-rated Best Pictures at IMDb in 2022 (eleven, not ten, because of several ties). The top eleven all ranked among IMDb's fifty highest-rated movies, while somehow the lowest-rated Best Picture had the same exact rating as *Deuce Bigelow: Male Gigolo* (1999) and actually trailed the 5.8/10 earned by *Police Academy 2* (1985). Rating a Best Picture winner down near the kind of movies that receive comments not heard since the *Hindenburg* explosion surely says more about the online voters (and their ages) than it does about *The Broadway Melody* (1929). Still, the rankings and ratings do provide interesting gauges of popular appreciation.

Incidentally, the ninety-five winners average a rating of 7.7/10, the exact number earned by ten Best Pictures, ranging from the earliest example, *Mutiny on the Bounty* (1935), to the latest, *Birdman or (The Unexpected Virtue of Ignorance)* (2014). *Titanic* (1997), the epic that topped our earlier list of "8 Greatest Movies of All Time," isn't included among the top 250 IMDb rankings, though it did beat the average rating with a robust 7.8/10.

ELEVEN HIGHEST-RATED BEST PICTURE WINNERS AT IMDB.COM (WITH RANKINGS)

1. **IMDb.com ranked #2: *The Godfather* (1972)**
- Rating = 9.2/10
2. **IMDb.com ranked #3: *The Godfather: Part II* (1974)**
- Rating = 9.0/10

3. **IMDb.com ranked #6: *Schindler's List* (1993)**
- Rating = 8.9/10
4. **IMDb.com ranked #7: *Lord of the Rings: The Return of the King* (2003)**

- Rating = 8.9/10
5. **IMDb.com ranked #12:** *Forrest Gump* **(1994)**
- Rating = 8.8/10
6. **IMDb.com ranked #18:** *One Flew Over the Cuckoo's Nest* **(1975)**
- Rating = 8.7/10
7. **IMDb.com ranked #21:** *The Silence of the Lambs* **(1991)**
- Rating = 8.6/10
8. **IMDb.com ranked #30:** *Parasite* **(2019)**
- Rating = 8.6/10
9. **IMDb.com ranked #44:** *Gladiator* **(2000)**
- Rating = 8.5/10
10. **IMDb.com ranked #45:** *The Departed* **(2006)**
- Rating = 8.5/10
11. **IMDb.com ranked #48:** *Casablanca* **(1942)**
- Rating = 8.4/10

ELEVEN LOWEST-RATED BEST PICTURE WINNERS AT IMDB.COM (NO RANKINGS)

1. *The Broadway Melody* **(1929)**
- Rating = 5.7/10
2. *Cavalcade* **(1933)**
- Rating = 5.9/10

3. ***Cimarron*** (1931)
- Rating = 6.0/10

4. ***Rebecca*** (1940)
- Rating = 6.0/10

5. ***Tom Jones*** (1963)
- Rating = 6.5/10

6. ***The Greatest Show on Earth*** (1952)
- Rating = 6.6/10

7. ***Gigi*** (1958)
- Rating = 6.7/10

8. ***The Great Ziegfeld*** (1936)
- Rating = 6.7/10

9. ***Around the World in 80 Days*** (1956)
- Rating = 6.8/10

10. ***Going My Way*** (1944)
- Rating = 7.1/10

11. ***Shakespeare in Love*** (1998)
- Rating = 7.1/10

How Green Was My Box Office: 15 Best Picture Winners That Were Also the Year's Top-Grossing Movie

Using the movie index provided by the-numbers.com, we've matched up the list of Best Picture winners with the list of global box-office champs to find where the two lists overlap. Shown below are the fifteen movies that appear on both lists.

The results are enlightening. For instance, in the first dozen years of Academy Awards ceremonies, a third of the Best Picture winners were also the most popular movies in the world. But in the last dozen years of Academy Awards ceremonies, *none* of the Best Picture winners were also the most popular movies. Additionally, four-fifths (80%) of the Best Picture/best box office champs are bunched up in the first five decades of the Academy Awards (the fiftieth ceremony was held in 1978). In contrast, only one movie this century, the last entry in *The Lord of the Rings* trilogy, reigned at both the Oscar ceremony and the box office.

So does this mean that mid-twentieth century audiences appreciated the sophisticated quality of Best Picture winners more than spectacle? Possibly, though there were certainly some spectacular effects-heavy box-office champs in the 1930s and '40s, including *King Kong* (1933) and *Samson and Delilah* (1949), that didn't even get a nomination for Best Picture, much less a win. Or could it be that twenty-first century audiences prefer movies with stories and characters they already know? Maybe that's why they've pushed multiple entries in the *Avengers, Harry Potter, Pirates of the Caribbean,* and *Star Wars* series to the top where they're far above unique, modestly successful Best Picture winners like *Moonlight* (2016) and *CODA* (2021), just to name two among many examples. Perhaps modern audiences simply prefer fun, cartoonish movies to munch popcorn by over thoughtful, challenging dramas to analyze. If any or all of these theories are true, then predicting future Best Picture winners should be easy. In short, don't expect the most popular movies to win, even if long ago they did.

1. *The Broadway Melody* (1929)
2. *It Happened One Night* (1934)
3. *You Can't Take It with You* (1938)
4. *Gone with the Wind* (1939)
5. *Going My Way* (1944)
6. *The Greatest Show on Earth* (1952)
7. *The Bridge on the River Kwai* (1957)
8. *Ben-Hur* (1959)
9. *Lawrence of Arabia* (1962)
10. *The Sound of Music* (1965)
11. *The Godfather* (1972)

12. *Rocky* (1976)

13. *Rain Man* (1988)

14. *Titanic* (1997)

15. *The Lord of the Rings: The Return of the King* (2003)

The Lord of the Rings: The Return of the King (2003).

100 Memorable Movies That Didn't Get Nominated for Best Picture

This list isn't about which Best Picture nominee should've won the Best Picture Oscar but didn't, so we're not inciting any arguments about how *Citizen Kane* (1941) was robbed by *How Green Was My Valley* (1941). Instead, we're pointing out that the following classics didn't even get *nominated* for Best Picture, which seems unfathomable, especially in years when there were ten or more nominations possible. If you really want to be shocked, see the list called "100 Memorable Movies with Zero Oscar Nominations" on page 40 for overlooked classics that didn't earn any kind of Oscar nomination at all, a list that includes some of the movies shown below.

In the following table, the left column presents a hundred overlooked movies that many people would think were worthy of Best Picture nominations. The right column presents Best Picture-nominated movies that had the year's fewest nominations. We're not suggesting that an overlooked movie on the left should automatically replace a nominee on the right. Just to compare a few movies from the 1970s, *Harold and Maude* wasn't a more qualified nominee in 1971 than *A Clockwork Orange*; *American Graffiti* doesn't have to yield to any of the 1973 movies on its immediate left; and 1977's *Close Encounters* over *Annie Hall*? No way. Still, the movies listed below do provide an interesting glimpse at the competition among Best Picture nominees from year to year.

Overlooked Movies (Year)	That Year's Best Picture Nominees with the Fewest Overall Nominations (Number)
1.-3. *City Lights*; *M*; *The Public Enemy* (all 1931)	*East Lynne* and *Trader Horn* (1)
4.-6. *Duck Soup*; *The Invisible Man*; *King Kong* (all 1933)	*She Done Him Wrong* and *Smilin' Through* (1)
7.-8. *The Bride of Frankenstein* and *A Night at the Opera* (both 1935)	*Ruggles of Red Gap* (1)
9. *Snow White and the Seven Dwarfs* (1937)	*Captains Courageous*, *Dead End*, and *Stage Door* (4)
10. *Bringing Up Baby* (1938)	*Grand Illusion* (1)
11.-12. *His Girl Friday* and *Pinocchio* (both 1940)	*All This, and Heaven Too* (3)
13.-16. *Laura*; *Meet Me in St. Louis*; *Thirty Seconds Over Tokyo*; *To Have and Have Not* (all 1944)	*Double Indemnity* and *Gaslight* (7)
17.-18. *The Big Sleep* and *Notorious* (both 1946)	*Henry V* and *The Razor's Edge* (4)

19. *Red River* (1948)	*The Treasure of the Sierra Madre* (4)
20.-21. *On the Town* and *White Heat* (both 1949)	*A Letter to Three Wives* (3)
22.-24. *The Asphalt Jungle* and *In a Lonely Place* (both 1950); *The Third Man* (1949)	*Father of the Bride* and *King Solomon's Mines* (3)
25. *The African Queen* (1951)	*Decision Before Dawn* (2)
26.-27. *The Bad and the Beautiful* and *Singin' in the Rain* (both 1952)	*Ivanhoe* (3)
28.-30. *Rear Window; A Star Is Born; 20,000 Leagues Under the Sea* (all 1954)	*Three Coins in the Fountain* (3)
31. *The Night of the Hunter* (1955)	*Mister Roberts* (3)
32. *The Searchers* (1956)	*Friendly Persuasion* (6)
33.-34. *Sweet Smell of Success* and *Paths of Glory* (both 1957)	*12 Angry Men* (3)
35.-36. *Touch of Evil* and *Vertigo* (both 1958)	*Auntie Mame* and *Cat on a Hot Tin Roof* (6)
37.-39. *North by Northwest; On the Beach; Some Like It Hot* (all 1959)	*Room at the Top* (6)
40.-41. *Psycho* and *Spartacus* (both 1960)	*Elmer Gantry* and *The Sundowners* (5)
42. *Splendor in the Grass* (1961)	*Fanny* (5)
43.-44. *The Man Who Shot Liberty Valance* and *The Manchurian Candidate* (both 1962)	*The Longest Day* (5)
45. *The Great Escape* (1963)	*America America* (4)
46.-47. *Cool Hand Luke* and *In Cold Blood* (both 1967)	*The Graduate* (7)

48.-49. *Rosemary's Baby* and *2001: A Space Odyssey* (1968)	*Rachel, Rachel* and *Romeo and Juliet* (4)
50. *They Shoot Horses, Don't They?* (1969)	*Z* (5)
51. *Little Big Man* (1970)	*Five Easy Pieces* (4)
52. *Harold and Maude* (1971)	*A Clockwork Orange* (4)
53.-55. *Badlands; Paper Moon; Serpico* (all 1973)	*American Graffiti, Cries and Whispers,* and *A Touch of Class* (5)
56. *The Man Who Would Be King* (1975)	*Jaws* (4)
57. *Close Encounters of the Third Kind* (1977)	*Annie Hall* (5)
58. *Days of Heaven* (1978)	*An Unmarried Woman* (3)
59.-61. *Alien; The China Syndrome; Manhattan* (all 1979)	*Norma Rae* (4)
62. *Star Wars: Episode V—The Empire Strikes Back* (1980)	*Ordinary People* and *Tess* (6)
63. *Body Heat* (1981)	*Atlantic City* (5)
64.-65. *Blade Runner* and *Sophie's Choice* (both 1982)	*Missing* (4)
66.-67. *Broadway Danny Rose* and *Once Upon a Time in America* (both 1984)	*A Soldier's Story* (3)
68.-69. *Back to the Future* and *The Purple Rose of Cairo* (both 1985)	*Kiss of the Spider Woman* (4)
70.-73. *Aliens; Blue Velvet; Hoosiers; Stand by Me* (all 1986)	*Children of a Lesser God* (5)
74. *Empire of the Sun* (1987)	*Hope and Glory* (5)
75. *Who Framed Roger Rabbit* (1988)	*Working Girl* (6)

76.-78. *Crimes and Misdemeanors; Do the Right Thing; When Harry Met Sally . . .* (all 1989)	*Field of Dreams* (3)
79.-81. *Miller's Crossing; The Grifters; The Hunt for Red October* (all 1990)	*Awakenings* (3)
82. *Thelma & Louise* (1991)	*Beauty and the Beast* (6)
83.-85. *Casino; Toy Story; The Usual Suspects* (all 1995)	*The Postman* (5)
86. *Boogie Nights* (1997)	*The Full Monty* (4)
87.-88. *Almost Famous* and *Requiem for a Dream* (both 2000)	*Chocolat, Erin Brockovich,* and *Traffic* (5)
89. *Frida* (2002)	*The Lord of the Rings: The Two Towers* (6)
90. *Match Point* (2005)	*Capote* and *Munich* (5)
91. *Pan's Labyrinth* (2006)	*Letters from Iwo Jima* and *Little Miss Sunshine* (4)
92.-93. *The Dark Knight* and *WALL-E* (both 2008)	*Frost/Nixon* and *The Reader* (5)
94. *Moonrise Kingdom* (2012)	*Beasts of the Southern Wild* (4)
95.-96. *Gone Girl* and *Interstellar* (both 2014)	*Selma* (2)
97. *Carol* (2015)	*Brooklyn* (3)
98. *I, Tonya* (2017)	*The Post* (2)
99. *Knives Out* (2019)	*Ford v Ferrari* (4)
100. *Spider-Man: No Way Home* (2021)	*CODA* and *Licorice Pizza* (3)

From Here to Inaccuracy: 8 Best Picture-Winning Movies with Typos in the Credits

While these next movies all won the Best Picture Oscar and so rank among the all-time best of the best, they're not flawless, as we discovered when we inspected their modern DVDs. We could've pointed out anachronisms accidentally shown in various Best Pictures, such as the white car in the background of a thirteenth century battle scene in *Braveheart* (1995). Or factual errors, as in *Titanic* (1997) when Leonardo DiCaprio ("Jack") mentions ice fishing at Wisconsin's Lake Wissota, even though that man-made reservoir wasn't created until five years *after* he went down with the ship.

Instead, we've concentrated on mistakes in the credits. Obviously these small imperfections in no way diminish the power of these classic movies, and most viewers never even notice them. For instance, audiences would have to be extremely attentive to catch the misspelling in the text at the end of *Spotlight* (2015), the movie shown below. Errors are still fun to find, however, and frankly they always surprise us, since the opening titles and closing credits are supposedly created at leisure with plenty of opportunities for corrections before the movie is released. You'd think so, anyway. Just to be fair, most of these movies came out long before spell-checking programs became ubiquitous. Also, to their credit the majority of Best Pictures have no errors or typos in the credits at all, so most times there's nothing that would be driving Miss Daisy crazy. Nevertheless, these next eight classics, great as they are, have one or two little text errors we couldn't resist pointing out.

1. *Annie Hall* (1977)
- In the final cast list at the ninety-two minute mark, "Duane Hall" is played by Christopher Wlaken, not the correct Walken.
- On the next card in the credits, the annoying "Joey Nichols" is played by Hy Ansel, not the correct Anzell.

2. ***Argo* (2012)**

- At 119 minutes, the TV show *Battlestar Galactica* is in the list of licensors, but it's misspelled as *Battlestar Gallactica*.

3. ***The Best Years of Our Lives* (1946)**

- Astonishingly, at 169 minutes the cast list misspells the name of one of the leads. Fredric March is shown incorrectly as Frederic March, even though his name was spelled correctly in the opening titles, and even though he was already a famous Hollywood star, a three-time Oscar nominee, and a Best Actor winner (he'd win again for this movie).

4. ***Casablanca* (1942)**

- Thirty seconds into the opening titles, the cast list misspells S.Z. Sakall as the incorrect S.K. Sakall (he's "Carl," the head waiter) and Madeleine Lebeau as the incorrect Madeleine LeBeau (she's "Yvonne," the rejected mistress).

5. ***Gone with the Wind* (1939)**

***Gone with the Wind* (1939).**

- Leading off "The Players" listed almost five minutes into the movie are two "At Tara," "Gerald O'Hara" and "Ellen, his wife." Barbara O'Neil is shown to be playing "Ellen," but unfortunately her last name gets misspelled as O'Neill, even though she was a prominent actress who would soon be nominated for *All This, and Heaven Too* (1940).

■ Next in the credits come "Scarlett's beaux," with George Reeves as "Brent Tarleton" and Fred Crane as "Stuart Tarleton." Actually, the reverse is true for the Tarleton twins: Reeves plays "Stuart" and Crane plays "Brent." This is made clear three minutes later in the movie's first scene when Reeves ("Stuart") says, "We want all your waltzes! First Brent, then me, then Brent, then me again, and so on."

6. *The Silence of the Lambs* **(1991)**

■ Almost five minutes into the movie we read a prominent sign that correctly spells Behavioral Science Services, but 112 minutes later the closing credits offer thanks to the FBI's Behavorial Science Unit.

7. *Spotlight* **(2015)**

■ About 121 minutes into the movie there's a long alphabetical list of 206 American and international cities. Granada, Spain is misspelled as Grenada.

Spotlight (2015).

8. *Unforgiven* **(1992)**

- More of a curiosity than a typo is "Bill Munny" in the closing credits. Dozens of times throughout the movie Clint Eastwood's lead character is called "William Munny" or, more frequently, simply "Will." However, at 129 minutes the character is spelled as "Bill Munny." Bill is a common nickname for William, of course, but that shortened form is never used for anyone other than "Little Bill," Gene Hackman's character.

15 Breakthroughs for the Best Picture Oscar

Fifteen notable milestones in the history of the Best Picture category.

1. **First movie to win for Best Picture once the category actually had that name**

Lawrence of Arabia **(1962)**

- At the first ceremony (held in 1929), *Wings* (1927) won for Outstanding Picture, a category we would now call Best Picture. However, Best Picture wasn't actually the category's official name until the thirty-fifth ceremony (held in 1963).

2. **First (and only) movie to win for Best Picture and be nominated in every other Oscar category it was eligible for**

Cimarron **(1931)**

- At the 1932 Oscar ceremony, *Cimarron* was eligible in seven categories and was nominated in all seven, winning three; it wasn't eligible in an eighth category, Best Writing (Original Story).
- By comparison, *Titanic* (1997), the co-record holder for the most nominations ever (fourteen), wasn't nominated in three

categories it was eligible for: Best Actor, Best Supporting Actor, and Best Writing.

3. First (and only) movie to win for Best Picture without being nominated for any other Oscars

Grand Hotel **(1932)**

- Two other movies won for Best Picture without *winning* any other Oscars: *The Broadway Melody* (1929) and *Mutiny on the Bounty* (1935).

4. First movie with sound to win for Best Picture

The Broadway Melody **(1929)**

- This was also the first musical to win for Best Picture.

5. First color movie to win for Best Picture

Gone with the Wind **(1939)**

- The first all-color movie nominated for Best Picture: *A Star Is Born* (1937).

6. First movie to win for Best Picture and for Best Actor, Best Actress, Best Director, and Best Writing

It Happened One Night **(1934)**

- This feat would later be achieved by *One Flew Over the Cuckoo's Nest* (1975) and *The Silence of the Lambs* (1991).

7. First animated movie nominated for Best Picture

Beauty and the Beast (1991)
- No animated movie has ever won for Best Picture.
- See the list called "3 Animated Movies Nominated for Best Picture" on page 504 for more on this topic.

8. First foreign language film nominated for Best Picture

Grand Illusion (1937)
- *Parasite* (2019) was the first movie in a foreign language (Korean) to win for Best Picture.

9. First horror film nominated for Best Picture

The Exorcist (1973)
- *The Silence of the Lambs* (1991) is usually considered to be the first horror movie to win for Best Picture.

10. First British production to win for Best Picture

Hamlet (1948)
- Among the later British productions to win for Best Picture: *Tom Jones* (1963), *Gandhi* (1982), *The English Patient* (1996), and *Slumdog Millionaire* (2008).

11. First (and only) movie based on something already shown on TV to win for Best Picture

Marty (1955)
- *Marty*, the original fifty-one-minute television play, was broadcast on *The Philco Television Playhouse* in 1953.

12. First (and only) X-rated movie to win for Best Picture

Midnight Cowboy (1969)
- Within a couple of years this movie was re-released with an R (Restricted) rating.
- *A Clockwork Orange* (1971) is the only other X-rated movie to get a Best Picture nomination; it too was later downgraded to an R.

13. First 3D movies nominated for Best Picture

Avatar (2009) and *Up* (2009)
- No 3D movie has ever won for Best Picture.

14. First sequel to win for Best Picture

The Godfather: Part II (1974)
- *The Lord of the Rings: The Return of the King* (2003) is the only other sequel to win for Best Picture.
- The first sequel nominated for Best Picture: *The Bells of St. Mary's* (1945), the follow-up to the Best Picture-winning *Going My Way* (1944).

15. First movie distributed by a streaming service to win for Best Picture

CODA (2021)
- Shown at the virtual Sundance Film Festival in January 2021, *CODA* was acquired for distribution by Apple TV+ and released online and in theaters eight months later.
- Another streaming service, Netflix, landed its first Best Picture nomination with *Roma* (2018); as of 2023 seven more Netflix movies have been nominated for the top Oscar, but none of them has ever won.

BEST ACTOR, ACTRESS, SUPPORTING ACTOR, AND SUPPORTING ACTRESS

7 Major Developments in the Best Actor and Best Actress Categories

Oscars for Best Actor and Best Actress have been handed out at every Academy Awards ceremony. These important categories have changed over the years, especially in the number of nominees, as explained below.

1. First ceremony (held in 1929)

The first time the Academy presented an Oscar for Best Actor, there were only two nominees; for Best Actress, only three nominees. What's more, the nominees were being recognized for their body of work, not for a single movie. Thus the Academy identified multiple movies, some of them from different years, along with the two winners.

- Best Actor: Emil Jannings, *The Way of All Flesh* (1927) and *The Last Command* (1928)
- Best Actress: Janet Gaynor, *7th Heaven* (1927); *Street Angel* (1928); and *Sunrise* (1927)

2. Second ceremony (held in 1930)

In the second year, the Academy announced no nominees, only winners, in its two acting categories. The Academy's subsequent research into its own "in-house records" revealed which movies, actors, and actresses "were under consideration." Besides the two winners shown below, four more actors and five more actresses were unofficial nominees at the second Oscar ceremony. Thinking she might win, Mary Pickford ordered a custom silk beaded gown from Paris long before the ceremony. When she accepted her award wearing the gown and conspicuous jewels, she launched a tradition of glamorous fashions for the Academy Awards.

- Best Actor: Warner Baxter, *In Old Arizona* (1928)
- Best Actress: Mary Pickford, *Coquette* (1929)

3. Third ceremony (held in 1930)

Though it was held in the same year as the second Oscar ceremony, the third ceremony showed further fluctuation in the Best Actress and Best Actress categories. Unlike the second ceremony, the third ceremony had actual nominees, five men for Best Actor and five women for Best Actress. The five-and-five nominees represented fifteen movies, however, not ten, because three actors and two actresses were nominated for two movies each. Norma Shearer accepted her award wearing the same glamorous gold lamé gown she'd worn in that winning movie.

- Best Actor: George Arliss, *Disraeli* (1929)
- Best Actress: Norma Shearer, *The Divorcee* (1930)

4. Fourth ceremony (held in 1931)

After the double acting nominations for George Arliss, Norma Shearer, and three others the previous year, the Academy limited nominees to one movie each, a rule that still applies. The number of Best Actor/Best Actress nominees at this ceremony was five per category, but that change wouldn't last long.

- Best Actor: Lionel Barrymore, *A Free Soul* (1931)
- Best Actress: Marie Dressler, *Min and Bill* (1930)

5. Fifth ceremony (held in 1932)

Seemingly stabilized at the fourth ceremony, the two acting categories immediately changed again the very next year. For the fifth ceremony the Academy announced only three nominees per category, a number that would continue to vary between three and six for the next three ceremonies.

- Best Actor: Wallace Beery, *The Champ* (1931) and Fredric March, *Dr. Jekyll* and *Mr. Hyde* (1931)
- Best Actress: Helen Hayes, *The Sin of Madelon Claudet* (1931)
- The Best Actor category at this fifth ceremony produced one of the rare ties in Academy Awards history. See the list called "10 Times When There Have Been Ties Between Multiple Winners" on page 31 for more on this topic.

6. Ninth ceremony (held in 1937)

After eight years of having only two categories for acting (Best Actor and Best Actress), the Academy added two more so that it could recognize superlative performances that came in smaller, shorter roles. To show that these new categories were still subordinate, however, the Academy gave these winners plaques, not golden statuettes, for the first six years, finally switching to actual Oscars at the sixteenth ceremony (held in 1944). The ninth ceremony also brought a commitment to the longstanding format that the Academy still uses for its acting awards: five different nominees per category, with each nominee named for one movie.

- Best Actor: Paul Muni, *The Story of Louis Pasteur* (1936)
- Best Actress: Luise Rainer, *The Great Ziegfeld* (1936)
- Best Supporting Actor: Walter Brennan, *Come and Get It* (1936)
- Best Supporting Actress: Gale Sondergaard, *Anthony Adverse* (1936)

7. Forty-ninth ceremony (held in 1977)

This is the ceremony when four decades of Oscar tradition changed. Instead of Best Actor and Best Actress as the names for the two main acting categories, the Academy started calling them Best Actor in a Leading Role and Best Actress in a Leading Role. Most people still use the original names, however, so we've retained them for these two list books whenever we refer to these categories. Similarly, we use Best Supporting Actor and Best Supporting Actress, which is what those two categories are commonly called even though the official names are (and always have been) Best Actor in a Supporting Role and Best Actress in a Supporting Role.

- Best Actor in a Leading Role: Peter Finch, *Network* (1976)
- Best Actress in a Leading Role: Faye Dunaway, *Network* (1976)

Men for All Seasons: 96 Best Actor Winners in Ninety-Five Ceremonies

The Oscar for Best Actor has been awarded at all ninety-five ceremonies since the first one in 1929, but there have actually been ninety-*six* Best Actor Oscars handed out. That's because of an obscure rule that affected the fifth awards ceremony (held in 1932). Fredric March technically had one more vote for Best Actor than runner-up Wallace Beery, but in its earliest years the Academy considered first- and second-place results within three votes of each other as basically a tie, and so both actors were presented with Oscars.

Eighty-five different actors have won the Best Actor Oscar (ten have won it more than once). These men are grouped together below by the number of nominations, and their winning movies are shown. Note that Emil Jannings' sole win is credited to two movies, not one; at the time, Oscars were awarded for a body of work, but later the voting procedure was adjusted so that each nomination was for only one movie from the previous year.

The longest streak of consecutive Best Actor nominations, by the way, was four in a row by Marlon Brando, spanning all the ceremonies from 1952 to 1955. With that streak Brando affected the acting profession in the 1950s the way the Beatles affected rock music in the 1960s and *Star Wars* (1977) affected pop culture in the 1970s—as a transcendent game-changer.

NINE BEST ACTOR NOMINATIONS

1. Laurence Olivier

- *Hamlet* (1948)

2. Spencer Tracy

- *Captains Courageous* (1937)
- *Boys Town* (1938)

EIGHT BEST ACTOR NOMINATIONS

3. Paul Newman

- *The Color of Money* (1986)

4. Jack Nicholson

- *One Flew Over the Cuckoo's Nest* (1975)
- *As Good as It Gets* (1997)

SEVEN BEST ACTOR NOMINATIONS

5. Marlon Brando

- *On the Waterfront* (1954)

- *The Godfather* (1972)

6. Dustin Hoffman

- *Kramer vs. Kramer* (1979)
- *Rain Man* (1988)

7. Jack Lemmon

- *Save the Tiger* (1973)

SIX BEST ACTOR NOMINATIONS

8. Daniel Day-Lewis

- *My Left Foot* (1989)
- *There Will Be Blood* (2007)
- *Lincoln* (2012)

9. Denzel Washington

- *Training Day* (2001)

There Will Be Blood (2007).

FIVE BEST ACTOR NOMINATIONS

10. Gary Cooper

- *Sergeant York* (1941)
- *High Noon* (1952)

11. Robert De Niro

- *Raging Bull* (1980)

12. Leonardo DiCaprio

- *The Revenant* (2015)

13. Tom Hanks

- *Philadelphia* (1993)
- *Forrest Gump* (1994)

14. Fredric March

- *Dr. Jekyll and Mr. Hyde* (1931)
- *The Best Years of Our Lives* (1946)

15. Paul Muni

- *The Story of Louis Pasteur* (1936)

16. Al Pacino

- *Scent of a Woman* (1992)

17. Gregory Peck

- *To Kill a Mockingbird* (1962)

18. Sean Penn

- *Mystic River* (2003)
- *Milk* (2008)

19. James Stewart

To Kill a Mockingbird (1962).

- *The Philadelphia Story* (1940)

FOUR BEST ACTOR NOMINATIONS

20. Burt Lancaster

- *Elmer Gantry* (1960)

THREE BEST ACTOR NOMINATIONS

21. Humphrey Bogart

- *The African Queen* (1951)

22. Jeff Bridges

- *Crazy Heart* (2009)

23. James Cagney

- *Yankee Doodle Dandy* (1942)

24. Ronald Colman

- *A Double Life* (1947)

25. Bing Crosby

- *Going My Way* (1944)

26. Russell Crowe

- *Gladiator* (2000)

27. Robert Duvall

- *Tender Mercies* (1983)

28. Clark Gable

- *It Happened One Night* (1934)

29. William Holden

- *Stalag 17* (1953)

30. Anthony Hopkins

- *The Silence of the Lambs* (1991)
- *The Father* (2020)

31. William Hurt

- *Kiss of the Spider Woman* (1985)

32. Charles Laughton

- *The Private Life of Henry VIII* (1933)

33. Gary Oldman

- *Darkest Hour* (2017)

34. Joaquin Phoenix

- *Joker* (2019)

35. Will Smith

- *King Richard* (2021)

36. Jon Voight

- *Coming Home* (1978)

Joker (2019).

TWO BEST ACTOR NOMINATIONS

37. George Arliss

- *Disraeli* (1929)

38. Wallace Beery

- *The Champ* (1931)

39. Nicolas Cage

- *Leaving Las Vegas* (1995)

40. Robert Donat

- *Goodbye, Mr. Chips* (1939)

41. Richard Dreyfuss

- *The Goodbye Girl* (1977)

42. José Ferrer

- *Cyrano de Bergerac* (1950)

43. Peter Finch

- *Network* (1976)

44. Colin Firth

- *The King's Speech* (2010)

45. Henry Fonda

- *On Golden Pond* (1981)

46. Alec Guinness

- *The Bridge on the River Kwai* (1957)

47. Gene Hackman

- *The French Connection* (1971)

48. Rex Harrison

- *My Fair Lady* (1964)

49. Ben Kingsley

- *Gandhi* (1982)

50. Sidney Poitier

- *Lilies of the Field* (1963)

51. Eddie Redmayne

- *The Theory of Everything* (2014)

52. Geoffrey Rush

- *Shine* (1996)

53. Maximilian Schell

- *Judgment at Nuremberg* (1961)

54. George C. Scott

- *Patton* (1970)

55. Rod Steiger

- *In the Heat of the Night* (1967)

56. John Wayne

- *True Grit* (1969)

True Grit (1969).

ONE BEST ACTOR NOMINATION

57. F. Murray Abraham

- *Amadeus* (1984)

58. Casey Affleck

- *Manchester by the Sea* (2016)

59. Lionel Barrymore

- *A Free Soul* (1931)

60. Warner Baxter

- *In Old Arizona* (1928)

61. Roberto Benigni

- *Life Is Beautiful* (1997)

62. Ernest Borgnine

- *Marty* (1955)

63. Adrien Brody

- *The Pianist* (2002)

64. Yul Brynner

- *The King and I* (1956)

The King and I (1956).

65. Art Carney

- *Harry and Tonto* (1974)

66. Broderick Crawford

- *All the King's Men* (1949)

67. Michael Douglas

- *Wall Street* (1987)

68. Jean Dujardin

- *The Artist* (2011)

69. Jamie Foxx

- *Ray* (2004)

70. Brendan Fraser

- *The Whale* (2022)

71. Charlton Heston

- *Ben-Hur* (1959)

The Whale (2022).

72. Philip Seymour Hoffman

- *Capote* (2005)

73. Jeremy Irons

- *Reversal of Fortune* (1990)

74. Emil Jannings

- *The Way of All Flesh* (1927) and *The Last Command* (1928)

75. Paul Lukas

- *Watch on the Rhine* (1943)

76. Rami Malek

- *Bohemian Rhapsody* (2018)

77. Lee Marvin

- *Cat Ballou* (1965)

78. Matthew McConaughey

- *Dallas Buyers Club* (2013)

79. Victor McLaglen

- *The Informer* (1935)

80. Ray Milland

- *The Lost Weekend* (1945)

The Lost Weekend (1945).

81. David Niven

- *Separate Tables* (1958)

82. Cliff Robertson

- *Charly* (1968)

83. Paul Scofield

- *A Man for All Seasons* (1966)

84. Kevin Spacey

- *American Beauty* (1999)

85. Forest Whitaker

- *The Last King of Scotland* (2006)

My Fair Ladies: 96 Best Actress Winners in Ninety-Five Ceremonies

As with the Best Actor category, the Best Actress Oscar has been awarded at ninety-five Academy Awards ceremonies since the first one in 1929, but there have actually been ninety-*six* Best Actress Oscars handed out, thanks to the famous tie at the 1969 ceremony between Katharine Hepburn and Barbra Streisand. Those ninety-six Oscars were won by seventy-nine different actresses (fourteen women have won more than one). Below, the seventy-nine are grouped together by the number of nominations and are followed by their winning movies. Note that Janet Gaynor's sole win is credited to three movies, not one; initially, Oscars were awarded for a body of work, but for the 1931 ceremony the voting procedure was adjusted so that each nomination was for only one movie from the previous year.

Interestingly, only two actresses, Katharine Hepburn and Luise Rainer, have won Best Actress Oscars in back-to-back years, which is the same number of actors who have won consecutive Best Actor Oscars (Spencer Tracy and Tom Hanks, as shown in the previous list). Two remarkable actresses bettered Marlon Brando's streak of four Best Actor nominations in a row with their own streaks of *five* consecutive Best Actress nominations: Bette Davis, at the 1939-1943 ceremonies, and Greer Garson, 1942-1946.

SEVENTEEN BEST ACTRESS NOMINATIONS

1. Meryl Streep

- *Sophie's Choice* (1982)
- *The Iron Lady* (2011)

TWELVE BEST ACTRESS NOMINATIONS

2. Katharine Hepburn

- *Morning Glory* (1933)
- *Guess Who's Coming to Dinner* (1967)
- *The Lion in Winter* (1968)
- *On Golden Pond* (1981)

TEN BEST ACTRESS NOMINATIONS

3. Bette Davis

- *Dangerous* (1935)
- *Jezebel* (1938)

SEVEN BEST ACTRESS NOMINATIONS

4. Greer Garson

- *Mrs. Miniver* (1942)

Mrs. Miniver (1942).

SIX BEST ACTRESS NOMINATIONS

5. Ingrid Bergman

- *Gaslight* (1944)
- *Anastasia* (1956)

6. Jane Fonda

- *Klute* (1971)
- *Coming Home* (1978)

7. Sissy Spacek

- *Coal Miner's Daughter* (1980)

FIVE BEST ACTRESS NOMINATIONS

8. Anne Bancroft

- *The Miracle Worker* (1962)

9. Cate Blanchett

- *Blue Jasmine* (2013)

Blue Jasmine (2013).

10. Ellen Burstyn

- *Alice Doesn't Live Here Anymore* (1974)

11. Susan Hayward

- *I Want to Live!* (1958)

12. Audrey Hepburn

- *Roman Holiday* (1953)

13. Jessica Lange

- *Blue Sky* (1994)

14. Shirley MacLaine

- *Terms of Endearment* (1983)

15. Susan Sarandon

- *Dead Man Walking* (1995)

16. Norma Shearer

- *The Divorcee* (1930)

17. Elizabeth Taylor

- *BUtterfield 8* (1960)
- *Who's Afraid of Virginia Woolf?* (1966)

FOUR BEST ACTRESS NOMINATIONS

18. Julie Christie

- *Darling* (1965)

19. Olivia de Havilland

- *To Each His Own* (1946)
- *The Heiress* (1949)

20. Glenda Jackson

- *Women in Love* (1969)
- *A Touch of Class* (1973)

21. Jennifer Jones

- *The Song of Bernadette* (1943)

22. Diane Keaton

- *Annie Hall* (1977)

The Heiress (1949).

23. Geraldine Page

- *The Trip to Bountiful* (1985)

24. Kate Winslet

- *The Reader* (2008)

25. Joanne Woodward

- *The Three Faces of Eve* (1957)

26. Jane Wyman

- *Johnny Belinda* (1948)

THREE BEST ACTRESS NOMINATIONS

27. Julie Andrews

- *Mary Poppins* (1964)

28. Claudette Colbert

- *It Happened One Night* (1934)

29. Joan Crawford

- *Mildred Pierce* (1945)

30. Faye Dunaway

- *Network* (1976)

31. Joan Fontaine

- *Suspicion* (1941)

32. Jodie Foster

- *The Accused* (1988)
- *The Silence of the Lambs* (1991)

33. Nicole Kidman

- *The Hours* (2002)

34. Jennifer Lawrence

- *Silver Linings Playbook* (2012)

35. Frances McDormand

- *Fargo* (1996)
- *Three Billboards Outside Ebbing, Missouri* (2017)
- *Nomadland* (2020)

36. Julianne Moore

- *Still Alice* (2014)

37. Charlize Theron

- *Monster* (2003)

38. Emma Thompson

- *Howards End* (1992)

39. Renée Zellweger

- *Judy* (2019)

TWO BEST ACTRESS NOMINATIONS

40. Sandra Bullock

- *The Blind Side* (2009)

41. Jessica Chastain

- *The Eyes of Tammy Faye* (2021)

42. Olivia Colman

- *The Favourite* (2018)

43. Marion Cotillard

- *La Vie en Rose* (2007)

44. Marie Dressler

- *Min and Bill* (1930)

45. Sally Field

- *Norma Rae* (1979)
- *Places in the Heart* (1984)

46. Janet Gaynor

- *7th Heaven* (1927); *Street Angel* (1928); and *Sunrise* (1927)

47. Holly Hunter

- *The Piano* (1993)

48. Vivien Leigh

- *Gone with the Wind* (1939)
- *A Streetcar Named Desire* (1951)

49. Sophia Loren

- *Two Women* (1960)

50. Anna Magnani

- *The Rose Tattoo* (1955)

51. Liza Minnelli

- *Cabaret* (1972)

52. Helen Mirren

- *The Queen* (2006)

53. Patricia Neal

- *Hud* (1963)

54. Natalie Portman

- *Black Swan* (2010)

55. Luise Rainer

- *The Great Ziegfeld* (1936)
- *The Good Earth* (1937)

56. Julia Roberts

- *Erin Brockovich* (2000)

57. Simone Signoret

- *Room at the Top* (1959)

58. Maggie Smith

- *The Prime of Miss Jean Brodie* (1969)

59. Barbra Streisand

- *Funny Girl* (1968)

60. Hilary Swank

- *Boys Don't Cry* (1999)
- *Million Dollar Baby* (2004)

61. Reese Witherspoon

- *Walk the Line* (2005)

62. Loretta Young

- *The Farmer's Daughter* (1947)

ONE BEST ACTRESS NOMINATION

63. Kathy Bates

- *Misery* (1990)

Monster's Ball (2001).

64. Halle Berry

- *Monster's Ball* (2001)

65. Shirley Booth

- *Come Back, Little Sheba* (1952)

66. Cher

- *Moonstruck* (1987)

67. Louise Fletcher

- *One Flew Over the Cuckoo's Nest* (1975)

68. Helen Hayes

- *The Sin of Madelon Claudet* (1931)

69. Judy Holliday

- *Born Yesterday* (1950)

70. Helen Hunt

- *As Good as It Gets* (1997)

71. Grace Kelly

- *The Country Girl* (1954)

72. Brie Larson

- *Room* (2015)

73. Marlee Matlin

- *Children of a Lesser God* (1986)

74. Gwyneth Paltrow

- *Shakespeare in Love* (1998)

75. Mary Pickford

- *Coquette* (1929)

76. Ginger Rogers

- *Kitty Foyle* (1940)

77. Emma Stone

- *La La Land* (2016)

78. Jessica Tandy

- *Driving Miss Daisy* (1989)

79. Michelle Yeoh

Everything Everywhere All at Once (2022).

- *Everything Everywhere All at Once* (2022)

Three Flew Over the Cuckoo's Nest: 3 Movies That Won Oscars for Best Actor, Best Actress, and Best Picture

On average, about once every thirty years a movie wins all three Oscars for Best Actor, Best Actress, and Best Picture. Those rare Best Pictures and their dynamic duos of Oscar-winning actors and actresses are shown below. Note how long it's been since Hollywood has pulled off this trifecta, so we're definitely due.

Incidentally, four movies have won Oscars for Best Actor and Best Actress without winning for Best Picture *Network* (1976); *Coming Home* (1978); *On Golden Pond* (1981); and *As Good as It Gets* (1997). Bonus points if you can name those winning leads without consulting the Appendix.

1. Clark Gable and Claudette Colbert, *It Happened One Night* (1934)
2. Jack Nicholson and Louise Fletcher, *One Flew Over the Cuckoo's Nest* (1975)
3. Anthony Hopkins and Jodie Foster, *The Silence of the Lambs* (1991)

12 Best Picture Winners with No Acting Nominations

A dozen movies have won the Oscar for Best Picture without getting a single nomination for an actor or actress in that movie. Hard to believe, especially when you consider someone like Gene Kelly in *An American in Paris* (1951) and wonder who else could have done everything he did in that Best Picture-winning musical—starring, choreographing, directing some sequences, even doing some of the stunts in a landmark movie that practically fizzes with his talent and energy—yet he wasn't even nominated. Every Best Picture winner without any acting nominations is shown below, grouped by the total number of nominations.

ELEVEN NOMINATIONS

1. *The Lord of the Rings: The Return of the King* (2003)

TEN NOMINATIONS

2. *Braveheart* (1995)
3. *Slumdog Millionaire* (2008)

NINE NOMINATIONS

4. *Gigi* (1958)
5. *The Last Emperor* (1987)

EIGHT NOMINATIONS

An American in Paris (1951).

6. *An American in Paris* (1951)
7. *Around the World in 80 Days* (1956)

SIX NOMINATIONS

8. *Parasite* (2019)

FIVE NOMINATIONS

9. *The Greatest Show on Earth* (1952)

FOUR NOMINATIONS

10. *All Quiet on the Western Front* (1930)

TWO NOMINATIONS

11. *Wings* (1927)

ONE NOMINATION

12. *Grand Hotel* (1932)

9 Movies with Five Acting Nominations

No movie has ever had six acting nominations, but nine movies have had five. The divine nine (and their nominated actors and actresses) are listed chronologically, with winners noted. Among the movies that just missed the cut with four acting nominations are heavyweights like *Gone with the Wind* (1939) and *The Godfather* (1972).

Incidentally, only three movies have ever won three acting Oscars: *A Streetcar Named Desire* (1951); *Network* (1976); and *Everything Everywhere All at Once* (2022).

Of the movies that received five acting nominations, only the two movies in the middle of the list were Oscarless for their acting. Four of the nine movies came out in the 1950s, an important decade for acting. Note too that no movie made after 1976 is in this pantheon of five acting nominations, though a few more recent movies, including *American Hustle* (2013) and *The Power of the Dog* (2021), came close with four acting nominations.

1. ***Mrs. Miniver* (1942)**
   - Best Actor: Walter Pidgeon
   - **Winner** Best Actress: Greer Garson
   - Best Supporting Actor: Henry Travers
   - Best Supporting Actress: May Whitty
   - **Winner** Best Supporting Actress: Teresa Wright
2. ***All About Eve* (1950)**
   - Best Actress: Anne Baxter
   - Best Actress: Bette Davis
   - **Winner** Best Supporting Actor: George Sanders
   - Best Supporting Actress: Celeste Holm
   - Best Supporting Actress: Thelma Ritter

***From Here to Eternity* (1953).**

3. *From Here to Eternity* **(1953)**
- Best Actor: Montgomery Clift
- Best Actor: Burt Lancaster
- Best Actress: Deborah Kerr
- **Winner** Best Supporting Actor: Frank Sinatra
- **Winner** Best Supporting Actress: Donna Reed

4. *On the Waterfront* **(1954)**
- **Winner** Best Actor: Marlon Brando
- Best Supporting Actor: Lee J. Cobb
- Best Supporting Actor: Karl Malden
- Best Supporting Actor: Rod Steiger
- Winner Best Supporting Actress: Eva Marie Saint

5. *Peyton Place* **(1957)**
- Best Actress: Lana Turner
- Best Supporting Actor: Arthur Kennedy
- Best Supporting Actor: Russ Tamblyn
- Best Supporting Actress: Hope Lange
- Best Supporting Actress: Diane Varsi

6. *Tom Jones* **(1963)**
- Best Actor: Albert Finney
- Best Supporting Actor: Hugh Griffith
- Best Supporting Actress: Diane Cilento
- Best Supporting Actress: Edith Evans
- Best Supporting Actress: Joyce Redman

7. *Bonnie and Clyde* **(1967)**
- Best Actor: Warren Beatty
- Best Actress: Faye Dunaway
- Best Supporting Actor: Gene Hackman
- Best Supporting Actor: Michael J. Pollard
- **Winner** Best Supporting Actress: Estelle Parsons

8. *The Godfather: Part II* **(1974)**
- Best Actor: Al Pacino
- **Winner** Best Supporting Actor: Robert De Niro
- Best Supporting Actor: Michael V. Gazzo
- Best Supporting Actor: Lee Strasberg
- Best Supporting Actress: Talia Shire

9. *Network* **(1976)**
- **Winner** Best Actor: Peter Finch
- Best Actor: William Holden
- **Winner** Best Actress: Faye Dunaway
- Best Supporting Actor: Ned Beatty
- **Winner** Best Supporting Actress: Beatrice Straight

12 Movies with Two Best Actor Nominees

Only twelve movies have had two actors nominated simultaneously for Best Actor. The dozen double-nominee movies are presented below chronologically, with the four winning actors noted. The first movie on the list even had *three* Best Actor nominees, but that head-to-head-to-head competition produced no winners. Watching some of these skillful teams operating together—the two *Sleuth* stars at number nine, for instance—is like watching an expert high-wire act minus the net.

If you're curious, twenty-one movies have had two Best Supporting Actor nominees. *Mr. Smith Goes to Washington* (1939) with Harry Carey and Claude Rains was the first movie with double Best Supporting Actor nominees; *The Banshees of Inisherin* (2022) with Brendan Gleeson and Barry Keoghan was the most recent example. *On the Waterfront* (1954) and *The Godfather* (1972) each had a trio of Best Supporting Actor nominees, though none of them won.

1. *Mutiny on the Bounty* (1935)
■   Clark Gable
■   Charles Laughton
■   Franchot Tone

2. *Going My Way* (1944)
■   **Winner** Bing Crosby
■   Barry Fitzgerald

3. *From Here to Eternity* (1953)
■   Montgomery Clift
■   Burt Lancaster

4. *Giant* (1956)
■   James Dean
■   Rock Hudson

5. *The Defiant Ones* (1958)
■   Tony Curtis
■   Sidney Poitier

6. ***Judgment at Nuremberg* (1961)**
- **Winner** Maximilian Schell
- Spencer Tracy

7. ***Becket* (1964)**
- Richard Burton
- Peter O'Toole

8. ***Midnight Cowboy* (1969)**
- Dustin Hoffman
- Jon Voight

9. ***Sleuth* (1972)**
- Michael Caine
- Laurence Olivier

10. ***Network* (1976)**
- **Winner** Peter Finch
- William Holden

11. ***The Dresser* (1983)**
- Tom Courtenay
- Albert Finney

12. ***Amadeus* (1984)**
- **Winner** F. Murray Abraham
- Tom Hulce

5 Movies with Two Best Actress Nominees

Only five movies have had two actresses nominated simultaneously for Best Actress. The five movies and ten actresses are shown below, with the one winner noted.

While it's rare for a movie to have two Best Actress nominees, it's far more common for a movie to have double nominees in the Best Supporting Actress category; as a matter of fact, that happened at five ceremonies in a row in the late 1940s and early '50s. Overall *thirty-six* movies have accomplished this Best Supporting double-nomination feat, starting with Olivia de Havilland and Hattie McDaniel (the eventual winner) in *Gone with the Wind* (1939) and continuing up to Jamie Lee Curtis (the winner) and Stephanie Hsu in *Everything Everywhere All at Once* (2022). *Tom Jones* (1963) actually had *three* Best Supporting Actress nominees—Diane Cilento, Edith Evans, and Joyce Redman—but they all lost to Margaret Rutherford in *The V.I.P.s* (1963).

1. *All About Eve* (1950)
- Anne Baxter
- Bette Davis
2. *Suddenly, Last Summer* (1959)
- Katharine Hepburn
- Elizabeth Taylor
3. *The Turning Point* (1977)
- Anne Bancroft
- Shirley MacLaine
4. *Terms of Endearment* (1983)
- **Winner** Shirley MacLaine
- Debra Winger
5. *Thelma & Louise* (1991)
- Geena Davis
- Susan Sarandon

4 Movies That Were Nominated for a Single Oscar—Best Actor—and Won

An acting performance must really stand out when it's the only aspect of the movie that the Academy recognizes. Below are the four chronologically listed movies that won when Best Actor was their sole nomination. The most recent, Forest Whitaker's portrayal of the brutal tyrant Idi Amin, was the kind of riveting performance so terrifying and real that it's impossible to forget, though you may wish you could.

1. José Ferrer, *Cyrano de Bergerac* (1950)
2. Cliff Robertson, *Charly* (1968)
3. Michael Douglas, *Wall Street* (1987)
4. Forest Whitaker, *The Last King of Scotland* (2006)

12 Movies That Were Nominated for a Single Oscar—Best Actress—and Won

Winning an Oscar when it's the only nomination the movie got might be more impressive than winning when the movie got many nominations. Consider the following dozen movies, none of which was an Oscar juggernaut that swept multiple categories; instead, the actresses made such an impression that the Academy couldn't *not* award them Best Actress Oscars.

The performances range from Marie Dressler's tough-but-lovable turn in the comedy/drama at number two to Joanne Woodward's versatile manifestations in the psychological study at number six. Number eleven on the list is a disturbing drama about a train wreck, with Charlize Theron utterly transformed into the hurtling train.

1. Mary Pickford, *Coquette* (1929)
2. Marie Dressler, *Min and Bill* (1930)
3. Helen Hayes, *The Sin of Madelon Claudet* (1931)
4. Katharine Hepburn, *Morning Glory* (1933)
5. Bette Davis, *Dangerous* (1935)
6. Joanne Woodward, *The Three Faces of Eve* (1957)
7. Sophia Loren, *Two Women* (1960)
8. Jodie Foster, *The Accused* (1988)
9. Kathy Bates, *Misery* (1990)

10. Jessica Lange, *Blue Sky* (1994)
11. Charlize Theron, *Monster* (2003)
12. Julianne Moore, *Still Alice* (2014)

5 Best Actor Winners Whose Winning Performance Came in a Musical

Recall some of the great musical stars in movies through the decades—Fred Astaire, Nelson Eddy, Howard Keel, Gene Kelly, Elvis Presley, Frank Sinatra, to name a half-dozen. None of them won an Oscar for performing in a musical. Astaire got a Best Supporting Actor nomination for his dramatic role in *The Towering Inferno* (1974); Kelly was a Best Actor nominee for a musical, *Anchors Aweigh* (1945); and Sinatra won the Best Supporting Actor Oscar for a drama, *From Here to Eternity* (1953). But Eddy, Keel, and Presley, along with many other musical stars, won no competitive statuettes for their performances in musicals. The five who did, all of them for Best Actor, are listed below.

Lee Marvin, who won the Best Actor Oscar for *Cat Ballou* (1965), isn't included; though that movie has musical narration, it's not really a musical, and Marvin himself goofily "sings" only about ten seconds of "Happy Birthday." Rami Malek's performance makes the list because, while he does lip synch in *Bohemian Rhapsody* (2018), he does it to a mix of voices, one of which is his own.

1. James Cagney, *Yankee Doodle Dandy* (1942)
2. Bing Crosby, *Going My Way* (1944)
3. Rex Harrison, *My Fair Lady* (1964)
4. Jamie Foxx, *Ray* (2004)
5. Rami Malek, *Bohemian Rhapsody* (2018)

9 Best Actress Winners Whose Winning Performance Came in a Musical

About 10 percent of the Oscar winners for Best Actress won the award for performing in a musical (coincidentally, that's approximately the same percentage of Best Picture-winning movies that were musicals).

We didn't include *The Country Girl* (1954) on the following list; even though Grace Kelly won the Best Actress Oscar, and even though songs are sung in the movie, none of them feature Kelly. The other actresses shown below really did sing their songs, however, which you'd expect for any movie with such musical powerhouses as Julie Andrews, Barbra Streisand, and Liza Minnelli, but maybe is a surprise for the movies starring Luise Rainer, Sissy Spacek, Reese Witherspoon, and Emma Stone, who weren't professional recording artists. Marion Cotillard just managed to sneak in; though she lip synched to Edith Piaf's voice for most of *La Vie en Rose* (2007), Cotillard is credited with co-singing one of the movie's songs herself.

1. Luise Rainer, *The Great Ziegfeld* (1936)
2. Julie Andrews, *Mary Poppins* (1964)
3. Barbra Streisand, *Funny Girl* (1968)
4. Liza Minnelli, *Cabaret* (1972)
5. Sissy Spacek, *Coal Miner's Daughter* (1980)
6. Reese Witherspoon, *Walk the Line* (2005)
7. Marion Cotillard, *La Vie en Rose* (2007)
8. Emma Stone, *La La Land* (2016)
9. Renée Zellweger, *Judy* (2019)

La La Land (2016).

6 Actors with at Least Four Best Actor Nominations and Zero Best Actor Wins

Previous lists have shown actors who won the Best Actor Oscar. This next list presents six actors who earned four or more nominations for Best Actor, and won none of them. Opening up the list to actors with three or more nominations would have added ten more names, including Montgomery Clift, Bradley Cooper, Kirk Douglas, Morgan Freeman, and Robin Williams. For the stars listed below, we follow with their first and last nominations so you can appreciate the span of these great careers. Peter O'Toole's nominations spread out across four-and-a-half decades, a remarkable achievement.

EIGHT BEST ACTOR NOMINATIONS

1. Peter O'Toole

- *Lawrence of Arabia* (1962)
- *Venus* (2006)

SIX BEST ACTOR NOMINATIONS

2. Richard Burton

- *The Robe* (1953)
- *Equus* (1977)

FOUR BEST ACTOR NOMINATIONS

3. Warren Beatty

- *Bonnie and Clyde* (1967)
- *Bugsy* (1991)

4. Charles Boyer

- *Conquest* (1937)
- *Fanny* (1961)

5. Michael Caine

- *Alfie* (1966)
- *The Quiet American* (2002)

6. Albert Finney

- *Tom Jones* (1963)
- *Under the Volcano* (1984)

9 Actresses with at Least Four Best Actress Nominations and Zero Best Actress Wins

Nine actresses earned four or more nominations for Best Actress without actually winning that award. Some of the stars shown below won separately for Best Supporting Actress—Judi Dench, for example—but none of them won for Best Actress. So that you can appreciate the span of these extraordinary careers, we've included each actress's first and last nominations. Note Glenn Close, whose nominations cover a thirty-year period, by far the longest on the list.

Just to name drop more great actresses, expanding the list to three nominations would add Annette Bening, Eleanor Parker, Saoirse Ronan, Gloria Swanson, Michelle Williams, and Debra Winger.

SIX BEST ACTRESS NOMINATIONS

1. Deborah Kerr

- *Edward, My Son* (1949)
- *The Sundowners* (1960)

FIVE BEST ACTRESS NOMINATIONS

2. Judi Dench

- *Mrs. Brown* (1997)
- *Philomena* (2013)

3. Irene Dunne

- *Cimarron* (1931)
- *I Remember Mama* (1948)

FOUR BEST ACTRESS NOMINATIONS

4. Glenn Close

- *Fatal Attraction* (1987)

- *The Wife* (2017)

5. Greta Garbo

- *Anna Christie* (1930)
- *Ninotchka* (1939)

6. Marsha Mason

- *Cinderella Liberty* (1973)
- *Only When I Laugh* (1981)

7. Vanessa Redgrave

- *Morgan: A Suitable Case for Treatment* (1966)
- *The Bostonians* (1984)

8. Rosalind Russell

- *My Sister Eileen* (1942)
- *Auntie Mame* (1958)

9. Barbara Stanwyck

- *Stella Dallas* (1937)
- *Sorry, Wrong Number* (1948)

4 Actors with Two Acting Nominations *in the Same Year*

Imagine the excitement of being nominated, not just for one acting Oscar, but for *two* at the same ceremony. That scenario has happened four times, but only one of these alphabetically listed actors actually competed against himself—that is, his performance in one movie was up against his performance in another one in the same category. That one-time occurrence involved the first actor on the list and happened one year before the Academy changed its rules to limit Best Actor nominations to one per actor per year.

The other actors on the list were nominated in two different acting categories, which meant that even if the actor lost for Best Supporting Actor (an award typically presented early in the Oscar ceremony), he could still hold out hope that he'd hear his name called near the end as the year's Best Actor. That's what happened with Al Pacino and Jamie Foxx at the 1993 and 2005 ceremonies, respectively. Barry Fitzgerald was in the unique position of being nominated for both Best Actor and Best Supporting Actor, not just in the same year, but for playing the same role in the same movie. This awkward anomaly was quickly corrected by the Academy so that a single performance could be in only one acting category, not two.

1. George Arliss

- **Winner** Best Actor: *Disraeli* (1929)
- Best Actor: *The Green Goddess* (1930)

2. Barry Fitzgerald

- Best Actor: *Going My Way* (1944)
- **Winner** Best Supporting Actor: *Going My Way* (1944)

3. Jamie Foxx

- **Winner** Best Actor: *Ray* (2004)
- Best Supporting Actor: *Collateral* (2004)

4. Al Pacino

- **Winner** Best Actor: *Scent of a Woman* (1992)
- Best Supporting Actor: *Glengarry Glen Ross* (1992)

10 Actresses with Two Acting Nominations *in the Same Year*

Double acting nominations in the same year have occurred much more frequently for actresses than for actors. As in the previous list about actors, only one of the alphabetically listed actresses shown below competed against herself with two simultaneous nominations in the same category. After Norma Shearer's two nominations (and one win) at the third Academy Awards ceremony (held in 1930), the Academy revised its rules so that no actress could be nominated more than once per year for Best Actress (a rule later applied to Best Supporting Actress as well). Thus the other nine actresses on the list were up for both Best Actress and Best Supporting Actress at the same ceremony.

No actress has won two acting Oscars in one year, and only four of those nine actresses managed to win in one of the two categories, as indicated. What's really impressive is the range displayed by some of these actresses who were playing wildly different characters but got nominations for both: Cate Blanchett at number two, for instance, with roles as a sixteenth century queen of England and a twentieth century king of music.

1. Fay Bainter

- Best Actress: *White Banners* (1938)
- **Winner** Best Supporting Actress: *Jezebel* (1938)

2. Cate Blanchett

- Best Actress: *Elizabeth, The Golden Age* (2007)
- Best Supporting Actress: *I'm Not There* (2007)

3. Holly Hunter

- **Winner** Best Actress: *The Piano* (1993)
- Best Supporting Actress: *The Firm* (1993)

4. Scarlett Johansson

- Best Actress: *Marriage Story* (2019)
- Best Supporting Actress: *Jojo Rabbit* (2019)

5. Jessica Lange

- Best Actress: *Frances* (1982)
- **Winner** Best Supporting Actress: *Tootsie* (1982)

6. Julianne Moore

- Best Actress: *Far from Heaven* (2002)
- Best Supporting Actress: *The Hours* (2002)

7. Norma Shearer

- **Winner** Best Actress: *The Divorcee* (1930)
- Best Actress: *Their Own Desire* (1929)

8. Emma Thompson

- Best Actress: *The Remains of the Day* (1993)
- Best Supporting Actress: *In the Name of the Father* (1993)

9. Sigourney Weaver

- Best Actress: *Gorillas in the Mist* (1988)
- Best Supporting Actress: *Working Girl* (1988)

10. Teresa Wright

- Best Actress: *The Pride of the Yankees* (1942)
- **Winner** Best Supporting Actress: *Mrs. Miniver* (1942)

9 Actors Whose Best Actor Nomination Was for a Performance in a Foreign Language

Even though the Academy had been honoring foreign-language films starring Toshirô Mifune, Jacques Tati and other international stars throughout the 1950s, no actor in a foreign-language movie was nominated for Best Actor until the 1960s.

The breakthrough was Marcello Mastroianni's nomination at the thirty-fifth Oscar ceremony (held in 1963). After that, Mastroianni, the clear leader in this group, got two more nominations, and eight other actors received Best Actor nominations for movies in which they predominately spoke a foreign language. The one winner in this category is noted.

FRENCH

1. Gérard Depardieu

- *Cyrano de Bergerac* (1990)

ITALIAN

2. Roberto Benigni

- **Winner** *Life Is Beautiful* (1997)

3. Giancarlo Giannini

- *Seven Beauties* (1975)

4. Marcello Mastroianni

- *Divorce Italian Style* (1961)
- *A Special Day* (1977)
- *Dark Eyes* (1987)

5. Massimo Troisi

- *The Postman* (1994)

KOREAN

6. Steven Yeun

- *Minari* (2020)

SPANISH

7. Antonio Banderas

- *Pain and Glory* (2019)

8. Javier Bardem

- *Biutiful* (2010)

SWEDISH

9. Max von Sydow

- *Pelle the Conqueror* (1987)

17 Actresses Whose Best Actress Nomination Was for a Performance in a Foreign Language

As in the previous list for actors, the Academy was slow to recognize foreign-language actresses and didn't nominate its first one until Melina Mercouri was up for Best Actress at the thirty-third ceremony (held in 1961). Thus Giulietta Masina, Maria Schell, and other stars of acclaimed international films in earlier decades were overlooked.

After Mercouri's breakthrough, the other actresses shown below all received Best Actress nominations for movies in which they predominately spoke a foreign language. Mercouri herself was a close call for the list; she spoke a lot of English in *Never on Sunday*, but she also conversed in Greek throughout the movie and sang the Oscar-winning theme song in her native tongue, so she's included here. Note Carol Kane at number seventeen: every other actress on the list was born in a foreign country, but Kane was born in Ohio. In her wise, charming movie, she conveyed remarkable growth without any overt histrionics, just with quiet Yiddish, subtle facial expressions, and the controlled strength of her steely determination.

FRENCH

1. Isabelle Adjani

- *The Story of Adele H.* (1975)
- *Camille Claudel* (1988)

2. Anouk Aimée

- *A Man and a Woman* (1966)

3. Marie-Christine Barrault

- *Cousin Cousine* (1975)

4. Marion Cotillard

- **Winner** *La Vie en Rose* (2007)
- *Two Days, One Night* (2014)

5. Catherine Deneuve

- *Indochine* (1992)

6. Isabelle Huppert

- *Elle* (2016)

7. Emmanuelle Riva

- *Amour* (2012)

GREEK

8. Melina Mercouri

- *Never on Sunday* (1960)

ITALIAN

9. Sophia Loren

- **Winner** *Two Women* (1960)
- *Marriage Italian Style* (1964)

PORTUGUESE

10. Fernanda Montenegro

- *Central Station* (1998)

SLOVAK

11. Ida Kamińska

- *The Shop on Main Street* (1965)

SPANISH

12. Yalitza Aparicio

- *Roma* (2018)

13. Penélope Cruz

- *Volver* (2006)
- *Parallel Mothers* (2021)

14. Catalina Sandino Moreno

- *Maria Full of Grace* (2004)

SWEDISH

15. Ingrid Bergman

- *Autumn Sonata* (1978)

16. Liv Ullmann

- *The Emigrants* (1971)
- *Face to Face* (1976)

YIDDISH

17. Carol Kane

- *Hester Street* (1975)

The Silence of the Silents: 4 Actors Who Won Oscars for Performances in Which They Barely Spoke

The following two lists present nine actors and actresses whose voices were rarely or never heard at all in the movies that won them Oscars. Why they barely spoke has varying explanations. First, the 1920s movies and *The Artist* (2011) were silent movies, so automatically they had no spoken dialogue. Second, the characters may have been literally unable to speak; to name two examples, John Mills in the list below was the mute supporting star in *Ryan's Daughter* (1970), and Jane Wyman in the list after this one was the mute lead star of *Johnny Belinda* (1948). However, even without speaking the following Oscar-winning actors and actresses were able to communicate volumes when voiced words couldn't.

BEST ACTOR

1. Jean Dujardin, *The Artist* (2011)

The Artist (2011).

2. Emil Jannings, *The Way of All Flesh* (1927) and *The Last Command* (1928)

BEST SUPPORTING ACTOR

3. John Mills, *Ryan's Daughter* (1970)
4. Troy Kotsur, *CODA* (2021)

5 Actresses Who Won Oscars for Performances in Which They Barely Spoke

In the previous list and this next one, note that multiple movies are shown for both Janet Gaynor and Emil Jannings. That's because in the Academy's early years the acting Oscar was given for a body of work, not just for a single movie.

All the actresses on the list won these Oscars when they were in their twenties or thirties, except for Patty Duke, who was only fifteen when her movie came out. Duke's character, the young Helen Keller, didn't speak because she had never learned how, having been struck deaf and blind from a severe case of scarlet fever when she was only nineteen months old.

BEST ACTRESS

1. Janet Gaynor, *7th Heaven* (1927); *Street Angel* (1928); and *Sunrise* (1927)
2. Holly Hunter, *The Piano* (1993)
3. Marlee Matlin, *Children of a Lesser God* (1986)
4. Jane Wyman, *Johnny Belinda* (1948)

BEST SUPPORTING ACTRESS

5. Patty Duke, *The Miracle Worker* (1962)

Patton Pending: 29 Actors Who Won the Best Actor Oscar for Playing a Real Person

Dozens of actors have gotten Best Actor nominations for playing real people whose names run the gamut from A to Z: A as in Muhammad Ali, played by Will Smith in *Ali* (2001); and Z as in Émile Zola, played by Paul Muni in *The Life of Emile Zola* (1937). Twenty-nine actors went to the next level by actually winning the Best Actor Oscar when playing a real person.

Not that the actors were doing an impersonation—barrel-chested George C. Scott spoke in a stern growl throughout *Patton* (1970), while the real-life general was a lean former Olympic runner who spoke in a high, thin voice, yet Scott's performance is still heralded as one of the most compelling screen portrayals ever. Also appreciate Daniel Day-Lewis, who won two Best Actor Oscars for playing two utterly different real people from two different centuries and two different countries.

1. F. Murray Abraham

- Antonio Salieri in *Amadeus* (1984)

2. George Arliss

- Benjamin Disraeli in *Disraeli* (1929)

3. Adrien Brody

- Władysław Szpilman in *The Pianist* (2002)

4. Yul Brynner

- King Mongkut of Siam in *The King and I* (1956)

5. James Cagney

- George M. Cohan in *Yankee Doodle Dandy* (1942)

6. Gary Cooper

- Alvin York in *Sergeant York* (1941)

7. Daniel Day-Lewis

- Christy Brown in *My Left Foot* (1989)
- Abraham Lincoln in *Lincoln* (2012)

8. Robert De Niro

- Jake LaMotta in *Raging Bull* (1980)

9. Leonardo DiCaprio

- Hugh Glass in *The Revenant* (2015)

10. José Ferrer

- Cyrano de Bergerac in *Cyrano de Bergerac* (1950)

11. Colin Firth

- King George VI in *The King's Speech* (2010)

12. Jamie Foxx

- Ray Charles in *Ray* (2004)

13. Gene Hackman

- Jimmy Doyle in *The French Connection* (1971)

The French Connection (1971).

14. Philip Seymour Hoffman

- Truman Capote in *Capote* (2005)

15. Jeremy Irons

- Claus von Bülow in *Reversal of Fortune* (1990)

16. Ben Kingsley

- Mahatma Gandhi in *Gandhi* (1982)

17. Charles Laughton

- King Henry VIII in *The Private Life of Henry VIII* (1933)

18. Rami Malek

- Freddie Mercury in *Bohemian Rhapsody* (2018)

19. Matthew McConaughey

- Ron Woodruff in *Dallas Buyers Club* (2013)

20. Paul Muni

- Louis Pasteur in *The Story of Louis Pasteur* (1936)

21. Gary Oldman

- Winston Churchill in *Darkest Hour* (2017)

22. Sean Penn

- Harvey Milk in *Milk* (2008)

23. Eddie Redmayne

- Stephen Hawking in *The Theory of Everything* (2014)

24. Geoffrey Rush

- David Helfgott in *Shine* (1996)

25. Paul Scofield

- Sir Thomas More in *A Man for All Seasons* (1966)

26. George C. Scott

- General George Patton in *Patton* (1970)

27. Will Smith

- Richard Williams in *King Richard* (2021)

28. Spencer Tracy

- Father Edward J. Flanagan in *Boys Town* (1938)

29. Forest Whitaker

- Idi Amin in *The Last King of Scotland* (2006)

Been-Her: 25 Actresses Who Won the Best Actress Oscar for Playing a Real Person

As in the previous list, a wide range of real people inspired the roles that led to Best Actress nominations. Some real people even inspired *two* nominated performances. Singer Billie Holiday, for example, was portrayed by two different nominated actresses, Diana Ross in *Lady Sings the Blues* (1972) and Andra Day in *The United States vs. Billie Holiday* (2021). Cate Blanchett even got two Best Actress nominations for playing the same real person, Queen Elizabeth I, in *Elizabeth* (1998) and *Elizabeth: The Golden Age* (2007).

Twenty-five portrayals of real people have culminated with Best Actress wins. This next list shows those actresses, the real people they played, and their movies.

1. Anne Bancroft

- Annie Sullivan in *The Miracle Worker* (1962)

2. Ingrid Bergman

- Anna Anderson ("Anna Koreff") in *Anastasia* (1956)

3. Sandra Bullock

- Leigh Anne Tuohy in *The Blind Side* (2009)

4. Jessica Chastain

- Tammy Faye Bakker in *The Eyes of Tammy Faye* (2021)

The Eyes of Tammy Faye (2021).

5. Olivia Colman

- Queen Anne in *The Favourite* (2018)

6. Marion Cotillard

- Édith Piaf in *La Vie en Rose* (2007)

7. Sally Field

- Crystal Lee Sutton ("Norma Rae Webster") in *Norma Rae* (1979)

8. Jodie Foster

- Cheryl Araujo ("Sarah Tobias") in *The Accused* (1988)

9. Susan Hayward

- Barbara Graham in *I Want to Live!* (1958)

10. Katharine Hepburn

- Eleanor of Aquitaine in *The Lion in Winter* (1968)

11. Jennifer Jones

- Bernadette Soubirous in *The Song of Bernadette* (1943)

12. Nicole Kidman

- Virginia Woolf in *The Hours* (2002)

13. Liza Minnelli

- Jean Ross ("Sally Bowles") in *Cabaret* (1972)

14. Helen Mirren

- Queen Elizabeth II in *The Queen* (2006)

15. Luise Rainer

- Anna Held in *The Great Ziegfeld* (1936)

16. Julia Roberts

- Erin Brockovich in *Erin Brockovich* (2000)

17. Susan Sarandon

- Helen Prejean in *Dead Man Walking* (1995)

18. Sissy Spacek

- Loretta Lynn in *Coal Miner's Daughter* (1980)

19. Meryl Streep

- Margaret Thatcher in *The Iron Lady* (2011)

20. Barbra Streisand

- Fanny Brice in *Funny Girl* (1968)

21. Hilary Swank

- Brandon Teena in *Boys Don't Cry* (1999)

22. Charlize Theron

- Aileen Wuornos in *Monster* (2003)

23. Reese Witherspoon

- June Carter in *Walk the Line* (2005)

24. Joanne Woodward

- Christine Costner ("Eve White"/"Eve Black"/"Jane") in *The Three Faces of Eve* (1957)

25. Renée Zellweger

- Judy Garland in *Judy* (2019)

7 Fictional Characters Who Generated Multiple Nominations for Best Actor

These seven fictional characters were played by different actors who all got Best Actor nominations (winners are noted). The actors underneath each fictional character are listed in their movies' chronological order to show who played the role first.

Not included are Al Pacino's performances as the fictional "Michael Corleone" character in *The Godfather* (1972) and *The Godfather: Part II* (1974) because that first one brought him a Best Supporting Actor nomination, not the sequel's Best Actor nomination. The reverse pattern applies to Sylvester Stallone, who's not included because his first "Rocky Balboa" nomination for *Rocky* (1976) was as Best Actor, and his second for *Creed* (2015) was as Best Supporting Actor. Note that Bing Crosby and Paul Newman actually played the same roles twice, getting nominations every time.

1. "Mr. Chipping"

- **Winner** Robert Donat, *Goodbye, Mr. Chips* (1939)
- Peter O'Toole, Goodbye, *Mr. Chips* (1969)

2. "Marshal 'Rooster' Cogburn"

- **Winner** John Wayne, *True Grit* (1969)
- Jeff Bridges, *True Grit* (2010)

3. "Eddie Felson"

- Paul Newman, *The Hustler* (1961)
- **Winner** Paul Newman, *The Color of Money* (1986)

4. "Professor Henry Higgins"

- Leslie Howard, *Pygmalion* (1938)
- **Winner** Rex Harrison, *My Fair Lady* (1964)

5. "Father O'Malley"

- **Winner** Bing Crosby, *Going My Way* (1944)
- Bing Crosby, *The Bells of St. Mary's* (1945)

6. "Joe Pendleton"

- Robert Montgomery, *Here Comes Mr. Jordan* (1941)
- Warren Beatty, *Heaven Can Wait* (1978)

7. "Norman Maine" (or "Jackson Maine")

- Fredric March ("Norman Maine"), *A Star Is Born* (1937)

- James Mason ("Norman Maine"), *A Star Is Born* (1954)
- Bradley Cooper ("Jackson Maine"), *A Star Is Born* (2018)

3 Fictional Characters Who Generated Multiple Nominations for Best Actress

These next sets of fictional characters were played by different actresses who all got Best Actress nominations, though none of them won. What juicy roles those are in *A Star Is Born*—no matter the decade or the century, and no matter what names are given to the main characters, the lead actors (as shown on the previous list) and the lead actresses can pretty much count on getting nominated. Well, not Kris Kristofferson and Barbra Streisand in the 1976 version, but three out of four movies with dual nominations isn't bad.

1. "Esther Blodgett" (or "Ally Maine")

- Janet Gaynor ("Esther Blodgett"), *A Star Is Born* (1937)
- Judy Garland ("Esther Blodgett"), *A Star Is Born* (1954)
- Lady Gaga ("Ally Maine"), *A Star Is Born* (2018)

2. "Leslie Crosbie"

- Jeanne Eagels, *The Letter* (1929)
- Bette Davis, *The Letter* (1940)

3. "Jo March"

- Winona Ryder, *Little Women* (1994)
- Saoirse Ronan, *Little Women* (2019)

5 Movies That Were Nominated for a Single Oscar—Best Supporting Actor—and Won

Ever since the Academy added two new Best Supporting categories at the ninth ceremony (held in 1937), five movies have showcased the winner in the Best Supporting Actor category when that was the movie's sole nomination. The five are shown below with the winning supporting actors.

At the sixty-fourth Academy Awards ceremony (held in 1992), Jack Palance's win at number four turned the seventy-three old actor into the biggest ham outside of a Hormel factory. To prove that older actors can do anything a younger actor can, Palance did one-arm pushups during his acceptance speech and then joked that he could do two-arm pushups all night long "whether she's there or not."

1. Walter Brennan, *Kentucky* (1938)
2. Van Heflin, *Johnny Eager* (1941)
3. Peter Ustinov, *Topkapi* (1964)
4. Jack Palance, *City Slickers* (1991)
5. Christopher Plummer, *Beginners* (2010)

8 Movies That Were Nominated for a Single Oscar—Best Supporting Actress—and Won

As with the previous list, these eight actresses must have really given startling performances for them to be singled out from movies that otherwise got zero nominations. Linda Hunt at number five is notable because her win was the first ever for an actress playing a male character.

1. Mary Astor, *The Great Lie* (1941)
2. Claire Trevor, *Key Largo* (1948)

3. Margaret Rutherford, *The V.I.P.s* (1963)
4. Goldie Hawn, *Cactus Flower* (1969)
5. Linda Hunt, *The Year of Living Dangerously* (1982)
6. Marisa Tomei, *My Cousin Vinny* (1992)
7. Angelina Jolie, *Girl, Interrupted* (1999)
8. Penélope Cruz, *Vicky Cristina Barcelona* (2008)

2 Actors with Four Best Supporting Actor Nominations and Zero Best Actor Nominations

Many actors have earned both Best Supporting Actor nominations and Best Actor nominations in their career. Jack Nicholson, for instance, has added four Best Supporting Actor nominations to his eight Best Actor nominations.

Some actors, however, excelled as supporting characters and got no Academy recognition for leading roles they might have played. The following actors are the only ones to receive four Best Supporting Actor nominations without ever getting a single Best Actor nomination. Their first and last nominations are included (with wins indicated).

1. Walter Brennan

- **Winner** *Come and Get It* (1936)
- *Sergeant York* (1941)

2. Claude Rains

- *Mr. Smith Goes to Washington* (1939)
- *Notorious* (1946)

5 Actresses with at Least Four Best Supporting Actress Nominations and Zero Best Actress Nominations

What the previous list does for actors, this next one does for actresses who earned four or more Best Supporting Actress nominations without ever being nominated for Best Actress. Some actresses have earned multiple nominations in both categories—Meryl Streep, an Oscar *machine*, has four Supporting nominations in addition to seventeen for Best Actress—but not these next five women who all thrived in supporting roles. Nominated and winning movies in this Best Supporting category are listed after the names.

Thelma Ritter, who leads this Oscar-nominated pack, usually played the same kind of acerbic, wise-cracking character. She got her six nominations in just thirteen years from some excellent movies, including one Best Picture winner, *All About Eve* (1950). But she herself never won; in fact, after she'd lost four years in a row in the 1950s she threw a "Come and Watch Me Lose Again" viewing party when she was nominated for *Pillow Talk* (1959).

SIX BEST SUPPORTING ACTRESS NOMINATIONS

1. Thelma Ritter

- *All About Eve* (1950)
- *Birdman of Alcatraz* (1963)

FOUR BEST SUPPORTING ACTRESS NOMINATIONS

2. Ethel Barrymore

- *Pinky* (1949)
- **Winner** *None But the Lonely Heart* (1944)

3. Lee Grant

- *Detective Story* (1951)
- *Voyage of the Damned* (1976)

4. Agnes Moorehead

- *The Magnificent Ambersons* (1942)
- *Hush . . . Hush, Sweet Charlotte* (1964)

5. Maureen Stapleton

- *Lonelyhearts* (1958)
- **Winner** *Reds* (1981)

3 Actors Who Won Oscars for Their First Performance

Each of the following actors made an instant impression on the Academy and won an Oscar for his first movie performance, which is listed after his name. All of them won in the same category, Best Supporting Actor. Interestingly, though all three were just starting their movie careers, none of them ever got another Oscar nomination in any category.

1. Timothy Hutton

- *Ordinary People* (1980)

2. Haing S. Ngor

- *The Killing Fields* (1984)

3. Harold Russell

- *The Best Years of Our Lives* (1946)

13 Actresses Who Won Oscars for Their First Performance

Budding talents bloomed quickly for the following actresses, each of whom won an Oscar for her first credited movie role. Unlike the three men in the previous list, some of the women listed below (Julie Andrews, Mercedes McCambridge, Gale Sondergaard, and Barbra Streisand) went on to later acting nominations (Andrews actually got two more).

While they were technically movie rookies, some of these actresses already had some minor acting experience, either from tiny, uncredited parts in movies or from appearances on TV. At age fourteen Julie Andrews, for instance, provided a singing voice for an animated Italian movie before becoming a stage star and then winning an Oscar for her first movie, *Mary Poppins* (1964); likewise, young Anna Paquin provided a voice for an animated Japanese movie before winning her Oscar at age eleven for her first screen role in *The Piano* (1993). Whatever their backgrounds, the following actresses all hit the big screen in a big way.

BEST ACTRESS

1. Julie Andrews

- *Mary Poppins* (1964)

2. Shirley Booth

- *Come Back, Little Sheba* (1952)

3. Marlee Matlin

- *Children of a Lesser God* (1986)

4. Barbra Streisand

- *Funny Girl* (1968)

BEST SUPPORTING ACTRESS

5. Jennifer Hudson

- *Dreamgirls* (2006)

6. Mercedes McCambridge

- *All the King's Men* (1949)

7. Lupita Nyong'o

- *12 Years a Slave* (2013)

8. Tatum O'Neal

- *Paper Moon* (1973)

9. Anna Paquin

- *The Piano* (1993)

The Piano (1993).

10. Katina Paxinou

- *For Whom the Bell Tolls* (1943)

11. Eva Marie Saint

- *On the Waterfront* (1954)

12. Gale Sondergaard

- *Anthony Adverse* (1936)

13. Jo Van Fleet

- *East of Eden* (1955)

12 Average Ages of Winners in the Acting Categories

Generally speaking, older actors are more likely to win Oscars than older actresses are. This holds for the two Best Actor/Best Actress Oscars and the two Best Supporting categories. And the trend, perhaps surprisingly, is going older. As shown below, in three of the four acting categories the winners today are older than the winners early in Academy Awards history.

The following list shows the average ages of winners in the four acting categories. The ages refer to the actors' and actresses' ages at the Academy Awards ceremonies when they were handed an Oscar (not their ages when they appeared in their nominated movies). Specific winning actors and actresses who were this exact average age (or closest to it) when they won their Oscars are also shown, with their ages in parentheses. The statistic for "average age for early three-decade periods" starts in the 1940s because the two supporting categories didn't have a complete decade of samples until that decade (the two categories were introduced in 1937).

BEST ACTOR

1. Winner's average age

Forty-four years old

- Emil Jannings (44), *The Last Command* (1928) and *The Way of All Flesh* (1927)
- Matthew McConaughey (44), *Dallas Buyers Club* (2013)

2. Winner's average age for early three-decade period

1940s-1960s: forty-two years old

- Lee Marvin (42), *Cat Ballou* (1965)
- Rod Steiger (42), *In the Heat of the Night* (1967)

In the Heat of the Night (1967).

3. Winner's average age for recent three-decade period

1990s-2010s: forty-five years old

- Geoffrey Rush (45), *Shine* (1996)
- Forest Whitaker (45), *The Last King of Scotland* (2006)

BEST ACTRESS

4. Winner's average age

Thirty-seven years old
- Glenda Jackson (37), *A Touch of Class* (1973)
- Mary Pickford (37), *Coquette* (1929)

5. Winner's average age for early three-decade period

1940s-1960s: thirty-five years old
- Elizabeth Taylor (35), *Who's Afraid of Virginia Woolf?* (1966)
- Loretta Young (35), *The Farmer's Daughter* (1947)

6. Winner's average age for recent three-decade period

1990s-2010s: thirty-nine years old
- Frances McDormand (39), *Fargo* (1996)

BEST SUPPORTING ACTOR

7. Winner's average age

Forty-nine years old
- Burl Ives (49), *The Big Country* (1958)
- Sam Rockwell (49), *Three Billboards Outside Ebbing, Missouri* (2017)

8. Winner's average age for early three-decade period

1940s-1960s: forty-seven years old
- Thomas Mitchell (47), *Stagecoach* (1939)

9. Winner's average age for recent three-decade period

1990s-2010s: fifty-one years old
- Chris Cooper (51), *Adaptation.* (2002)

BEST SUPPORTING ACTRESS

10. Winner's average age

Forty-one years old
- Marcia Gay Harden (41), *Pollock* (2000)
- Vanessa Redgrave (41), *Julia* (1977)
- Octavia Spencer (41), *The Help* (2011)
- Jo Van Fleet (41), *East of Eden* (1955)

11. Winner's average age for early three-decade period

1940s-1960s: forty years old
- Estelle Parsons (40), *Bonnie and Clyde* (1967)

12. Winner's average age for recent three-decade period

1990s-2010s: thirty-eight years old
- Rachel Weisz (35), *The Constant Gardener* (2005)
- Marcia Gay Harden (41), *Pollock* (2000)

No Oscars for Old Men: 17 Children Nominated for Acting Oscars

Given the vague interpretations of the age that defines a child, we'll apply one used by the Department of Motor Vehicles. In two-thirds of American states, teens can legally drive with a restricted license when they're fifteen years old. Consequently, the next seventeen actors and actresses were too young to drive—in some cases, *way* too young—when they were nominated for competitive Oscars. "Competitive Oscars" means we're not including the Special Award presented as a "Juvenile Oscar" to a dozen children and teenagers, starting with six-year-old Shirley Temple at the seventh ceremony (held in 1935) and ending with fourteen-year-old Hayley Mills at the thirty-third ceremony (held in 1961).

Note that it's easier to get an Oscar nomination or a win as a young actress than as a young actor. Not only are there over three times as many actresses on the list (thirteen vs. four), there are two winning actresses, whereas no young actors won. The ages given, from youngest to oldest, are the actors' and actresses' ages when their movies first came out. The movies they were nominated for follow the names, with the two winners identified.

BEST ACTOR

1. Jackie Cooper (8)

- *Skippy* (1931)

BEST ACTRESS

2. Quvenzhané Wallis (8)

- *Beasts of the Southern Wild* (2012)

3. Keisha Castle-Hughes (12)

- *Whale Rider* (2002)

BEST SUPPORTING ACTOR

4. Justin Henry (8)

- *Kramer vs. Kramer* (1979)

Kramer vs. Kramer (1979).

5. Brandon De Wilde (11)

- *Shane* (1953)

6. Haley Joel Osment (11)

- *The Sixth Sense* (1999)

BEST SUPPORTING ACTRESS

7. Abigail Breslin (9)

- *Little Miss Sunshine* (2006)

8. Tatum O'Neal (9)

- **Winner** *Paper Moon* (1973)

***Paper Moon* (1973).**

9. Mary Badham (10)

- *To Kill a Mockingbird* (1962)

10. Quinn Cummings (10)

- *The Goodbye Girl* (1977)

11. Anna Paquin (10)

- **Winner** *The Piano* (1993)

12. Patty McCormack (11)

- *The Bad Seed* (1956)

13. Jodie Foster (13)

- *Taxi Driver* (1976)

14. Bonita Granville (13)

- *These Three* (1936)

15. Saoirse Ronan (13)

- *Atonement* (2007)

16. Linda Blair (14)

- *The Exorcist* (1973)

17. Hailee Steinfeld (14)

- *True Grit* (2010)

10 Nominations for Acting When the Actors Were Eighty Years Old or Older

The following actors got Oscar nominations for their acting after they were four-fifths of a century old. The impressive list includes legendary names like Duvall, Hopkins, and von Sydow. George Burns in *The Sunshine Boys* (1975) and Al Pacino in *The Irishman* (2019) are among the famous actors who just missed the cut at age seventy-nine.

Note that Christopher Plummer is on the list *three* times for performances in his eighties, and as of 2021 Anthony Hopkins (eighty-three) became the oldest Best Actor nominee and winner, replacing the previous record-holder, Henry Fonda (76), who won for *On Golden Pond* (1980). Golden years, indeed. Ages, from oldest to youngest, show how old each actor was in the year his movie came out. Nominated movies are under the names, with winning performances identified.

BEST ACTOR

1. Anthony Hopkins (83)

- **Winner** *The Father* (2020)

BEST SUPPORTING ACTOR

2. Christopher Plummer (88)

- *All the Money in the World* (2017)

3. Judd Hirsch (87)

- *The Fabelmans* (2022)

4. Robert Duvall (83)

- *The Judge* (2014)

5. Hal Holbrook (82)

- *Into the Wild* (2007)

6. Anthony Hopkins (82)

- *The Two Popes* (2019)

7. Ralph Richardson (82)

- *Greystoke: The Legend of Tarzan, Lord of the Apes* (1984)

8. Max von Sydow (82)

- *Extremely Loud & Incredibly Close* (2011)

9. Christopher Plummer (81)

- **Winner** *Beginners* (2010)

10. Christopher Plummer (80)

- *The Last Station* (2009)

8 Nominations for Acting When the Actresses Were Eighty Years Old or Older

It's easier to get an Oscar nomination as an older actor than as an older actress. If you compare the previous list with this next one, you'll observe that there were more Oscar-nominated actors who were eighty or older than there were nominated actresses in that age range. More Oscar winners, too, with two winning actors and only one winning actress. Similar results come if the ages are extended to seventy-five years or older: twenty-two nominated actors (including seven winners) would make that list, but only seventeen actresses (with two winners) would qualify. The lesson for actresses is that whenever possible they should try not to get any older, because Hollywood seems to value youth over age (gee, ya think?).

Among the actresses, just missing the cut at age seventy-nine are two Best Actress nominees, Judi Dench in *Philomena* (2013) and Edith Evans in *The Whisperers* (1967); Evans actually had *three*

Oscar nominations in her mid-to-late seventies. And consider Gloria Stuart, born two years *before* the historic sinking shown eight decades later in *Titanic* (1997). Ages, from oldest to youngest, show how old each actress was in the year her movie was released. Nominated movies are under the names, with the one winning performance called out.

BEST ACTRESS

1. Jessica Tandy (80)

- **Winner** *Driving Miss Daisy* (1989)

BEST SUPPORTING ACTRESS

2. Judi Dench (87)

- *Belfast* (2021)

3. Gloria Stuart (87)

- *Titanic* (1997)

4. Ruby Dee (85)

- *American Gangster* (2007)

5. Emmanuelle Riva (85)

- *Amour* (2012)

6. June Squibb (84)

- *Nebraska* (2013)

7. Jessica Tandy (82)

- *Fried Green Tomatoes* (1991)

8. Eva Le Gallienne (81)

- *Resurrection* (1980)

Going My Weigh: 10 Actors Who Gained or Lost at Least Forty Pounds for Their Oscar-Nominated Roles

The next two lists present fourteen actors and actresses who endured serious physical changes to play their Oscar-nominated (and sometimes Oscar-winning) roles. As amazing as some of these huge weight gains are, maybe what's even more amazing is that these stars then lost that weight. Christian Bale is on the list *twice*, making him the perfect spokesperson for Duncan yo-yos.

There are other notable performances involving severe weight gain or weight loss—Vincent D'Onofrio's addition of seventy pounds for *Full Metal Jacket* (1987), for instance—but since they weren't nominated for those movies they're not included in this next list. Nominated movies follow the actors' names, with winners noted.

GAINED SIXTY POUNDS

1. Robert De Niro

- **Winner** Best Actor: *Raging Bull* (1980)

GAINED FIFTY POUNDS

2. Russell Crowe

- Best Actor: *The Insider* (1999)

GAINED FORTY POUNDS

3. Christian Bale

- Best Actor: *American Hustle* (2013)
- Best Actor: *Vice* (2018)

4. Bradley Cooper

- Best Actor: *American Sniper* (2014)

LOST SIXTY POUNDS

5. Denzel Washington

- Best Actor: *The Hurricane* (1999)

LOST FIFTY POUNDS

6. Joaquin Phoenix

- **Winner** Best Actor: *Joker* (2019)

7. Tom Hanks

- Best Actor: *Cast Away* (2000)

LOST FORTY POUNDS

8. Jonah Hill

- Best Supporting Actor: *Moneyball* (2011)

9. Philip Seymour Hoffman

- **Winner** Best Actor: *Capote* (2005)

10. Matthew McConaughey

- **Winner** Best Actor: *Dallas Buyers Club* (2013)

4 Actresses Who Gained Thirty Pounds for Their Oscar-Nominated Roles

As seen in the previous list, some meaty roles require serious weight gain. These next four actresses all added thirty or more pounds for their Oscar-nominated (and sometimes Oscar-winning) performances. Charlize Theron gained *fifty* pounds for *Tully* (2018), but that wasn't an Oscar-nominated role so it's not shown below.

We couldn't find any examples of Oscar-nominated actresses who lost thirty pounds for their Oscar-nominated/Oscar-winning roles, though Anne Hathaway, who slimmed down by approximately twenty-five pounds for *Les Misérables* (2012), came close. Nominated movies follow the actresses' names, with winners noted.

1. Elizabeth Taylor

- **Winner** Best Actress: *Who's Afraid of Virginia Woolf?* (1966)

2. Charlize Theron

- **Winner** Best Actress: *Monster* (2003)

3. Shelley Winters

- **Winner** Best Supporting Actress: *The Diary of Anne Frank* (1959)
- Best Supporting Actress: *The Poseidon Adventure* (1972)

4. Renée Zellweger

- Best Actress: *Bridget Jones's Diary* (2001)

25 Famous Actors Who Never Got an Oscar Nomination

Undoubtedly every movie fan could add someone to this list. Some of the names listed below are real head-scratchers—we're still not sure how the Academy could overlook Steve Buscemi as a Best Supporting Actor nominee for *Fargo* (1996), or Malcolm McDowell as a Best Actor nominee for *A Clockwork Orange* (1971), or John Goodman, who's never been bad in anything. Some of the actors below did get acknowledged with an Honorary Award—Steve Martin, for example—but we're listing stars who were never nominated in a competitive Oscar category.

1. Kevin Bacon
2. John Barrymore
3. Steve Buscemi
4. Jim Carrey
5. Joseph Cotten
6. John Cusack
7. Errol Flynn
8. Glenn Ford
9. Richard Gere
10. John Goodman
11. Hugh Grant
12. Alan Ladd
13. Peter Lorre
14. Steve Martin
15. Malcolm McDowell
16. Ewan McGregor
17. Tyrone Power
18. Dennis Quaid
19. Edward G. Robinson
20. Kurt Russell
21. Martin Sheen
22. Donald Sutherland
23. John Turturro
24. Eli Wallach
25. Bruce Willis

25 Famous Actresses Who Never Got an Oscar Nomination

There are some surprising names on this list of actresses who were never nominated for a competitive acting Oscar. Consider Marilyn

Monroe, the fuzzy end of the lollipop and nothing from the Academy for *Some Like It Hot* (1959). Then there's Meg Ryan, faking one of Hollywood's most famous comedic scenes in *When Harry Met Sally . . .* (1989), yet not even nominated. That just seems wrong. Maureen O'Hara is among the actresses shown below who did get acknowledged with an Honorary Award, but this list is about stars who were never nominated in a competitive Oscar category.

1. Ellen Barkin
2. Emily Blunt
3. Claire Danes
4. Cameron Diaz
5. Angie Dickinson
6. Mia Farrow
7. Pam Grier
8. Jean Harlow
9. Rita Hayworth
10. Myrna Loy
11. Ida Lupino
12. Andie MacDowell
13. Marilyn Monroe
14. Demi Moore
15. Kim Novak
16. Catherine O'Hara
17. Maureen O'Hara
18. Christina Ricci
19. Isabella Rossellini
20. Jane Russell
21. Rene Russo
22. Meg Ryan
23. Shirley Temple
24. Kerry Washington
25. Robin Wright

Some Like It Hot (1959).

14 Favorite Movies with Memorable Acting Performances, Selected by Oscar-Nominee Candy Clark

She's best known for her Oscar-nominated performance in George Lucas's delightful *American Graffiti* (1973)—she played "Debbie," the fun-loving Connie Stevens/Sandra Dee lookalike with a pile of platinum blonde hair and an enthusiasm for hot cars—but Candy Clark has also been in many other notable movies. Born in Oklahoma and raised in Texas, Candy was a New York fashion model when she landed her first movie role in *Fat City* (1972), the John Huston drama she calls "an underrated treasure," and soon she was co-starring with David Bowie in *The Man Who Fell to Earth* (1976) and Robert Mitchum in *The Big Sleep* (1978). Over the next four decades dozens of movies and TV shows followed, among them prominent movies directed by such luminaries as John Badham, Jonathan Demme, David Fincher, David Lynch, Nicolas Roeg, and Steven Soderbergh (visit her website candyclarkactor.com for the impressive list).

Today Candy lives and works in Los Angeles, she's as lively as ever, and she's still a person who knows how to tell an entertaining story. We asked about her favorite movies with memorable acting performances, and she gave us this chronologically ordered list of entertaining classics that every student of film acting needs to see.

1. *Psycho* (1960)
2. *What Ever Happened to Baby Jane?* (1962)
3. *The Birds* (1963)
4. *Who's Afraid of Virginia Woolf?* (1966)
5. *Midnight Cowboy* (1969)
6. *A Clockwork Orange* (1971)
7. *American Graffiti* (1973)
8. *The Exorcist* (1973)
9. *Chinatown* (1974)
10. *Network* (1976)
11. *Taxi Driver* (1976)
12. *Midnight Express* (1978)
13. *Scarface* (1983)
14. *Don't Look Up* (2021)

9 Breakthroughs for the Best Actor and Best Actress Oscars

Notable milestones among the nominees and winners for the Best Actor and Best Actress Oscars.

1. First actor and actress to win for a performance in a foreign-language film

Best Actor: Roberto Benigni

- Italy's *Life Is Beautiful* (1997)
- No other actor in a foreign-language film has won the Best Actor Oscar.

Best Actress: Sophia Loren

- Italy's *Two Women* (1960)
- Marion Cotillard later won the Best Actress Oscar for *La Vie en Rose* (2007), becoming the only other actress to win her Best Actress Oscar for a performance in a foreign language (French).

2. First actor and actress to win for a performance in a musical

Best Actor: James Cagney
- *Yankee Doodle Dandy* (1942)
- See the list called "5 Best Actor Winners Whose Winning Performance Came in a Musical" on page 203 for more on this topic.

Best Actress: Luise Rainer
- *The Great Ziegfeld* (1936)
- See the list called "9 Best Actress Winners Whose Winning Performance Came in a Musical" on page 204 for more on this topic.

3. First Best Actor and Best Actress winners who played LGBT characters

Best Actor: William Hurt
- *Kiss of the Spider Woman* (1985)

Best Actress: Hilary Swank
- *Boys Don't Cry* (1999)

4. First Black performers to win for Best Actor and Best Actress

Sidney Poitier
- *Lilies of the Field* (1963)

Halle Berry
- *Monster's Ball* (2001)
- Hattie McDaniel was the first Black performer to win an Oscar: Best Supporting Actress, *Gone with the Wind* (1939).

5. First actor and actress to win two Best Actor and Best Actress Oscars

Best Actor: Spencer Tracy
- *Captains Courageous* (1937)
- *Boys Town* (1938)
- These wins made Tracy the first winner of two consecutive Best Actor Oscars, a feat Tom Hanks later duplicated: *Philadelphia* (1993) and *Forrest Gump* (1994).

Best Actress: Luise Rainer
- *The Great Ziegfeld* (1936)
- *The Good Earth* (1937)
- Rainer was also the first winner of two consecutive Best Actress Oscars, a feat Katharine Hepburn later duplicated: *Guess Who's Coming to Dinner* (1967) and *The Lion in Winter* (1968).

6. First actor and actress to win three Best Actor and Best Actress Oscars

Best Actor: Daniel Day-Lewis
- *My Left Foot* (19989)
- *There Will Be Blood* (2007)
- *Lincoln* (2012)
- No other actor has won more than two Best Actor Oscars.

Best Actress: Katharine Hepburn
- *Morning Glory* (1933)
- *Guess Who's Coming to Dinner* (1967)
- *The Lion in Winter* (1968)
- *On Golden Pond* (1981)
- Frances McDormand is the only other three-time Best Actress winner.

7. First Best Actor and Best Actress winners not in attendance to receive their Oscars

Emil Jannings
- *The Way of All Flesh* (1927) and *The Last Command* (1928)
- Jannings was already scheduled to return to Europe before the first Academy Awards ceremony (held in 1929), so the Academy gave him his Best Actor Oscar early, making him the first "no show" winner.

Katharine Hepburn
- *Morning Glory* (1933)
- Hepburn didn't show up to receive any of her four Best Actress Oscars (listed above).

8. First Best Actor or Best Actress winner to refuse his/her Oscar

George C. Scott
- Refusing to accept his Best Actor Oscar for *Patton* (1970), Scott was a defiant "no show" at the forty-third ceremony (held in 1971).

Patton (1970).

- No actress has refused her Best Actress Oscar.

9. Youngest and oldest Best Actor or Best Actress winners

Marlee Matlin (21)

- *Children of a Lesser God* (1986)
- Adrien Brody (29) is the youngest Best Actor winner: *The Pianist* (2002).

Anthony Hopkins (83)
- *The Father* (2020)
- Jessica Tandy (80) was the oldest Best Actress winner: *Driving Miss Daisy* (1989).

6 Major Developments in the Best Director Category

The Best Director category took almost a decade to settle in with the standardized terms and number of nominees we still use today. Here are a half-dozen early developments as the Best Director category evolved. We've included the first winners after each change was made.

1. First ceremony (held in 1929)

The first time the Best Director Oscar was presented, it was given to two directors for two classifications of movies, comedies (with three nominated directors) and dramas (two nominees).

- Best Director (Comedy Picture): Lewis Milestone, *Two Arabian Knights* (1927)
- Best Director (Dramatic Picture): Frank Borzage, *7th Heaven* (1927)

2. Second ceremony (held in 1930)

For the ceremony's second year, the Academy combined the two classifications into a single Best Director category; there were six nominees (actually five, because Frank Lloyd was nominated twice).

- Best Director: Frank Lloyd, *The Divine Lady* (1928)

3. Third ceremony (held in 1930)

The number of Best Director nominees was changed to five.

- Best Director: Lewis Milestone, *All Quiet on the Western Front* (1930)

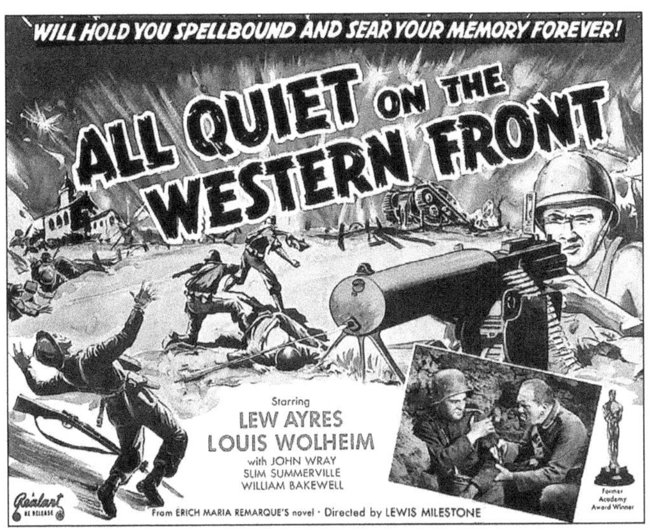

4. Fifth ceremony (held in 1932)

Starting with the fifth ceremony and continuing for the next three years, the number of Best Director nominees dropped to three.

- Best Director: Frank Borzage, *Bad Girl* (1931)

5. Ninth ceremony (held in 1937)

The Academy standardized the number of Best Director nominees at five, the number still used today. Unlike the Best Actor and Best Actress categories, where nobody can be nominated more than once per year, today it is still possible for one director to be nominated twice in the same year; see the list called "4 Directors Nominated for Best Director Twice *in the Same Year*" on page 289 for the double nominees.

- Best Director: Frank Capra, *Mr. Deeds Goes to Town* (1936)

6. Thirty-fourth ceremony (held in 1962)

For the first time co-directors of one movie were nominated for Best Director. See the list called "5 Times Co-Directors of One Movie Were Nominated for Best Director" on page 294 for other directing tandems.

- Best Directors: Jerome Robbins and Robert Wise, *West Side Story* (1961)

27 Times When the Best Director Winner Didn't Match the Best Picture Winner

At sixty-eight of the ninety-five Academy Awards ceremonies, the Best Director Oscar has gone to the person who directed that year's Best Picture. This means that when viewers watch the Oscars on TV, they can use the Best Director winner to accurately predict the Best Picture winner 71% of the time. Instead of showing the sixty-eight perfect matches between the two categories, this next list presents the other twenty-seven times when the movies represented by these two important Oscars *didn't* match. Under each ceremony are the Best Director winner and the Best Picture winner. John Ford is the only director to appear on this list three times.

One of the biggest upsets on the list is shown at number eleven, where the surprise Best Picture winner, the musical *An American in Paris* (1951), came from back in the pack to nose out two heavily favored dramas: *A Place in the Sun* (1951), which won for Best Director, and *A Streetcar Named Desire* (1951), which had the most nominations.

1. First ceremony (held in 1929)

- Best Director (Comedy Picture): Lewis Milestone, *Two Arabian Knights* (1927)

- Best Director (Dramatic Picture): Frank Borzage, *7th Heaven* (1927)
- Best Picture: *Wings* (1927)

2. Second ceremony (held in 1930)

- Best Director: Frank Lloyd, *The Divine Lady* (1928)
- Best Picture: *The Broadway Melody* (1929)

3. Fourth ceremony (held in 1931)

- Norman Taurog, *Skippy* (1931)
- *Cimarron* (1931)

4. Fifth ceremony (held in 1932)

- Frank Borzage, *Bad Girl* (1931)
- *Grand Hotel* (1932)

5. Eighth ceremony (held in 1936)

- John Ford, *The Informer* (1935)
- *Mutiny on the Bounty* (1935)

6. Ninth ceremony (held in 1937)

- Frank Capra, *Mr. Deeds Goes to Town* (1936)
- *The Great Ziegfeld* (1936)

7. Tenth ceremony (held in 1938)

- Leo McCarey, *The Awful Truth* (1937)
- *The Great Ziegfeld* (1936)

8. Thirteenth ceremony (held in 1941)

- John Ford, *The Grapes of Wrath* (1940)
- *Rebecca* (1940)

9. Twenty-first ceremony (held in 1949)

- John Huston, *The Treasure of the Sierra Madre* (1948)
- *Hamlet* (1948)

10. Twenty-second ceremony (held in 1950)

- Joseph L. Mankiewicz, *A Letter to Three Wives* (1949)
- *All the King's Men* (1949)

11. Twenty-fourth ceremony (held in 1952)

- George Stevens, *A Place in the Sun* (1951)
- *An American in Paris* (1951)

12. Twenty-fifth ceremony (held in 1953)

- John Ford, *The Quiet Man* (1952)
- *The Greatest Show on Earth* (1952)

The Greatest Show on Earth (1952).

13. Twenty-ninth ceremony (held in 1957)

- George Stevens, *Giant* (1956)
- *Around the World in 80 Days* (1956)

14. Fortieth ceremony (held in 1968)

- Mike Nichols, *The Graduate* (1967)
- *In the Heat of the Night* (1967)

15. Forty-fifth ceremony (held in 1973)

- Bob Fosse, *Cabaret* (1972)
- *The Godfather* (1972)

16. Fifty-fourth ceremony (held in 1982)

- Warren Beatty, *Reds* (1981)
- *Chariots of Fire* (1981)

17. Sixty-second ceremony (held in 1990)

- Oliver Stone, *Born on the Fourth of July* (1989)
- *Driving Miss Daisy* (1989)

18. Seventy-first ceremony (held in 1999)

- Steven Spielberg, *Saving Private Ryan* (1998)
- *Shakespeare in Love* (1998)

19. Seventy-third ceremony (held in 2001)

- Steven Soderbergh, *Traffic* (2000)
- *Gladiator* (2000)

20. Seventy-fifth ceremony (held in 2003)

- Roman Polanski, *The Pianist* (2002)
- *Chicago* (2002)

21. Seventy-eighth ceremony (held in 2006)

- Ang Lee, *Brokeback Mountain* (2005)
- *Crash* (2004)

22. Eighty-fifth ceremony (held in 2013)

- Ang Lee, *Life of Pi* (2012)
- *Argo* (2012)

23. Eighty-sixth ceremony (held in 2014)

- Alfonso Cuarón, *Gravity* (2013)
- *12 Years a Slave* (2013)

24. Eighty-eighth ceremony (held in 2016)

- Alejandro G. Iñárritu, *The Revenant* (2015)
- *Spotlight* (2015)

25. Eighty-ninth ceremony (held in 2017)

- Damien Chazelle, *La La Land* (2016)
- *Moonlight* (2016)

26. Ninety-first ceremony (held in 2019)

- Alfonso Cuarón, *Roma* (2018)
- *Green Book* (2018)

27. Ninety-fourth ceremony (held in 2022)

- Jane Campion, *The Power of the Dog* (2021)
- *CODA* (2021)

6 Best Picture Winners with No Directing Nomination

This next list shows the six Best Picture-winning movies that didn't get a nomination for Best Director.

Hold on—hasn't science proven that great movies are great because of great direction? Ninety-five Best Picture winners, eighty-nine of them with Best Director nominations. That's a near-perfect 94%. Again, science. So did these next six movies direct themselves? Seems like it, since the Academy didn't even acknowledge the directors with a nomination but did declare their movies to be the year's best. Here are the six winning movies and their un-nominated directors.

1. William Wellman, *Wings* (1927)
2. Edmund Goulding, *Grand Hotel* (1932)
3. Bruce Beresford, *Driving Miss Daisy* (1989)
4. Ben Affleck, *Argo* (2012)
5. Peter Farrelly, *Green Book* (2018)

Green Book (2018).

6. Siân Heder, *CODA* (2021)

1 Movie That Was Nominated for a Single Oscar—Best Director—and Won

It seems unlikely that a movie's director would get nominated for Best Director without the acting, or any other aspect of the movie, getting additional nominations. Yet that exact scenario happened fourteen times and involved such prominent directors as Robert Altman, Federico Fellini, David Lynch, Martin Scorsese, and King Vidor.

The only one of these fourteen occasions when the director actually won the Best Director Oscar came at the very first Academy Awards ceremony (held in 1929). This was the only ceremony to have separate Best Director categories for comedies and dramas;

Lewis Milestone's win was the only Oscar ever presented for Best Director (Comedy Picture), and it represented his movie's only nomination.

1. Lewis Milestone, *Two Arabian Knights* (1927)

26 Directors with at Least Four Best Director Nominations

The next five lists provide the background information for a sixth list of the greatest directors of all time. First up is a list of Best Director nominations. As impressive as the following list is—and it *is* impressive, featuring some of the greatest directors of all time—notice who is not on the list. Not one woman—not Kathryn Bigelow, Jane Campion, Greta Gerwig, Lina Wertmüller, or any other prominent female director—because only Campion got more than a single directing nomination (she got two). And no Black directors—is that possible, Spike Lee never got another directing nomination besides *BlacKkKlansman* (2018)? Baffling, but true.

Consider too the all-star directors who just missed the cut with three directing nominations, among them Paul Thomas Anderson, Ingmar Bergman, Bob Fosse, Roman Polanski, Ridley Scott, and Quentin Tarantino. James Cameron, Alfonso Cuarón, William Friedkin, Peter Jackson, and Vincente Minnelli are in the group with two directing nominations, and Peter Bogdanovich, Victor Fleming, Howard Hawks, Herbert Ross, and François Truffaut got only one nomination each. Somehow Tim Burton, Charles Chaplin, Brian De Palma, John Hughes, Rob Reiner, and some other prominent names got no Best Director nominations at all. Enough about who's not on the list; here's who is.

TWELVE BEST DIRECTOR NOMINATIONS

1. William Wyler

NINE BEST DIRECTOR NOMINATIONS

2. Martin Scorsese
3. Steven Spielberg

EIGHT BEST DIRECTOR NOMINATIONS

4. Billy Wilder

SEVEN BEST DIRECTOR NOMINATIONS

5. Woody Allen
6. David Lean
7. Fred Zinnemann

SIX BEST DIRECTOR NOMINATIONS

8. Frank Capra

FIVE BEST DIRECTOR NOMINATIONS

9. Robert Altman
10. Clarence Brown
11. George Cukor
12. John Ford
13. Alfred Hitchcock
14. John Huston
15. Elia Kazan
16. George Stevens
17. King Vidor

FOUR BEST DIRECTOR NOMINATIONS

18. Francis Ford Coppola
19. Clint Eastwood
20. Federico Fellini
21. Stanley Kubrick
22. Frank Lloyd
23. Sidney Lumet
24. Joseph L. Mankiewicz
25. Mike Nichols
26. Peter Weir

21 Directors with at Least Two Best Director Wins

Continuing with our run-up to the list of the greatest directors of all time, we move to winners of the Best Director Oscar. Below are the two-time winners of this important award, along with their winning movies. Be sure to appreciate Frank Capra's achievement on the following list: Capra, the first director to get above-the-title credit, won an Oscar every other year in the mid-1930s, giving him three in a five-year span.

As with the previous list of Best Director nominations, it's hard to believe who's not on this list of two-time Best Director winners. Francis Ford Coppola, George Cukor, Michael Curtiz, Bob Fosse, John Huston, Vincente Minnelli, Mike Nichols, Sydney Pollack, Martin Scorsese, Oliver Stone, and many others—not here, because they won only one Best Director Oscar. And consider the directors who never won at all, despite getting multiple nominations. Some of them are so famous you'll recognize them by just their last names: Bergman, Fellini, Hitchcock, Kubrick, Tarantino, among others. Nominations, yes, but actual Best Director Oscars, no.

FOUR BEST DIRECTOR WINS

1. John Ford

- *The Informer* (1935)
- *The Grapes of Wrath* (1940)
- *How Green Was My Valley* (1941)
- *The Quiet Man* (1952)

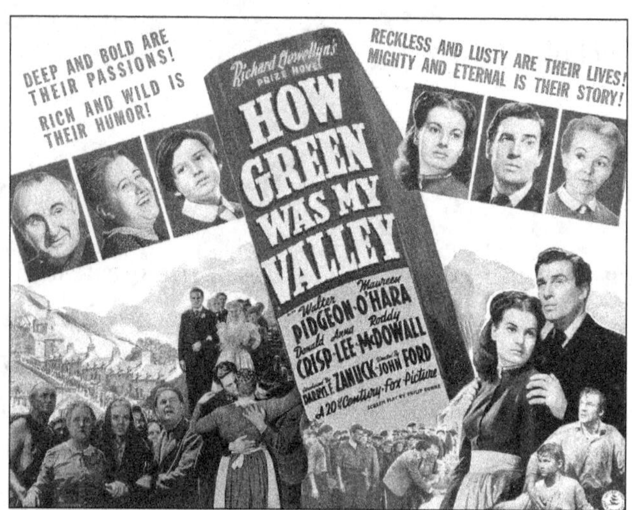

THREE BEST DIRECTOR WINS

2. Frank Capra

- *It Happened One Night* (1934)
- *Mr. Deeds Goes to Town* (1936)
- *You Can't Take It with You* (1938)

3. William Wyler

- *Mrs. Miniver* (1942)
- *The Best Years of Our Lives* (1946)
- *Ben-Hur* (1959)

TWO BEST DIRECTOR WINS

4. Frank Borzage

- *7th Heaven* (1927)
- *Bad Girl* (1931)

5. Alfonso Cuarón

- *Gravity* (2013)
- *Roma* (2018)

6. Clint Eastwood

- *Unforgiven* (1992)
- *Million Dollar Baby* (2004)

7. Miloš Forman

- *One Flew Over the Cuckoo's Nest* (1975)
- *Amadeus* (1984)

8. Alejandro G. Iñárritu

- *Birdman or (The Unexpected Virtue of Ignorance)* (2014)
- *The Revenant* (2015)

9. Elia Kazan

- *Gentleman's Agreement* (1947)
- *On the Waterfront* (1954)

10. David Lean

- *The Bridge on the River Kwai* (1957)
- *Lawrence of Arabia* (1962)

11. Ang Lee

- *Brokeback Mountain* (2005)
- *Life of Pi* (2012)

12. Frank Lloyd

- *The Divine Lady* (1928)
- *Cavalcade* (1933)

13. Joseph L. Mankiewicz

- *A Letter to Three Wives* (1949)
- *All About Eve* (1950)

14. Leo McCarey

- *The Awful Truth* (1937)
- *Going My Way* (1944)

15. Lewis Milestone

- *Two Arabian Nights* (1927)
- *All Quiet on the Western Front* (1930)

16. Steven Spielberg

- *Schindler's List* (1993)
- *Saving Private Ryan* (1998)

17. George Stevens

- *A Place in the Sun* (1951)
- *Giant* (1956)

18. Oliver Stone

- *Platoon* (1986)
- *Born on the Fourth of July* (1989)

19. Billy Wilder

- *The Lost Weekend* (1945)
- *The Apartment* (1960)

20. Robert Wise

- *West Side Story* (1961)
- *The Sound of Music* (1965)

21. Fred Zinnemann

- *From Here to Eternity* (1953)
- *A Man for All Seasons* (1966)

13 Directors Who Directed at Least Six Best Picture Nominees

Another way to gauge a director's career is to count how many Best Picture-nominated movies he or she directed. These thirteen legendary directors represent 104 Best Picture nominations, which average out to eight Best Picture nominations each. The directors are shown with their first and last Best Picture nominees. Look at how long some of these spans are for nominated Best Pictures—forty-seven years for Steven Spielberg, forty-three for Martin Scorsese. Consider too who just missed the cut with five nominations for Best Picture, notables like Francis Ford Coppola, Clint Eastwood, and Billy Wilder, and also note some of the famous names with four nominations, including Alfred Hitchcock, Ang Lee, and Quentin Tarantino.

Hidden in this list of nominees are two remarkable streaks: from the late 1930s to the early 1940s, William Wyler directed a Best Picture nominee at *seven* consecutive ceremonies, while in the same time period Frank Capra directed Best Picture nominees at four consecutive ceremonies.

THIRTEEN BEST PICTURE NOMINEES

1. William Wyler

- *Dodsworth* (1936)
- *Funny Girl* (1968)

2. Steven Spielberg

- *Jaws* (1975)
- *The Fabelmans* (2022)

NINE BEST PICTURE NOMINEES

3. John Ford

- *Arrowsmith* (1931)
- *How the West Was Won* (1962)

4. Martin Scorsese

- *Taxi Driver* (1976)
- *The Irishman* (2019)

EIGHT BEST PICTURE NOMINEES

5. Mervyn LeRoy

- *Five Star Final* (1931)
- *Mister Roberts* (1955)

SEVEN BEST PICTURE NOMINEES

6. Frank Capra

- *Lady for a Day* (1933)
- *It's a Wonderful Life* (1946)

7. George Cukor

- *Little Women* (1933)
- **Winner** *My Fair Lady* (1964)

8. Henry King

- *State Fair* (1933)
- *It's a Wonderful Life* (1946)

9. George Stevens

- *Alice Adams* (1935)
- *The Diary of Anne Frank* (1959)

SIX BEST PICTURE NOMINEES

10. Michael Curtiz

- *Captain Blood* (1935)
- *Mildred Pierce* (1945)

11. David Lean

- *In Which We Serve* (1942)
- *A Passage to India* (1984)

12. Sam Wood

- *Goodbye, Mr. Chips* (1939)
- *For Whom the Bell Tolls* (1943)

13. Fred Zinnemann

- *High Noon* (1952)
- *Julia* (1977)

12 Directors Who Directed at Least Two Best Picture Winners

If you've been reading the previous lists about famous directors and their Oscar achievements, you'll recognize the names on this next list. It shows the dozen directors who made two or more movies that won the Oscar for Best Picture, with their winning movies shown. In that phrase "two or more," there's only one person who qualifies as "or more," and he leads off the list.

As you'll see, Clint Eastwood is the only director who made one of his Best Picture winners in the twenty-first century. In fact, of the twenty-five movies listed below, twenty-one were made before the 1980s.

THREE BEST PICTURE WINNERS

1. William Wyler

- *Mrs. Miniver* (1942)
- *The Best Years of Our Lives* (1946)

The Best Years of Our Lives **(1946).**

- *Ben-Hur* (1959)

TWO BEST PICTURE WINNERS

2. Frank Capra

- *It Happened One Night* (1934)
- *You Can't Take It with You* (1938)

3. Francis Ford Coppola

- *The Godfather* (1972)
- *The Godfather: Part II* (1974)

4. Clint Eastwood

- *Unforgiven* (1992)
- *Million Dollar Baby* (2004)

5. Miloš Forman

- *One Flew Over the Cuckoo's Nest* (1975)
- *Amadeus* (1984)

6. Elia Kazan

- *Gentleman's Agreement* (1947)
- *On the Waterfront* (1954)

7. David Lean

- *The Bridge on the River Kwai* (1957)
- *Lawrence of Arabia* (1962)

8. Frank Lloyd

- *Cavalcade* (1933)
- *Mutiny on the Bounty* (1935)

9. Vincente Minnelli

- *An American in Paris* (1951)
- *Gigi* (1958)

10. Billy Wilder

- *The Lost Weekend* (1945)
- *The Apartment* (1960)

11. Robert Wise

- *West Side Story* (1961)
- *The Sound of Music* (1965)

12. Fred Zinnemann

- *From Here to Eternity* (1953)
- *A Man for All Seasons* (1966)

10 Directors Whose Movies Generated the Most Acting Nominations and Oscars

So far we have gauged directors' legacies by adding up how many Best Director Oscars he or she was personally nominated for and won. On that basis, William Wyler's total of fifteen (twelve nominations and three wins) puts him first, just ahead of Martin Scorsese and Billy Wilder, who each totaled ten. We've also counted Best

Picture nominations and wins for the directors, and by both measures Wyler again comes out on top.

Another important measure would be to count the number of competitive Oscar nominations and wins earned by the actors and actresses in each director's movies, based on the valid assumption that a director should get credit for generating acting nominations and wins. Based on the totals shown below, Wyler once more finishes first, with Scorsese a distant third. Here are the ten directors whose movies generated the most Oscar nominations and wins for actors and actresses. Not shown is Herbert Ross, whose movies generated a dozen acting nominations and two wins, plus one remarkable statistic worth noting: Ross's *The Goodbye Girl* (1977) and *The Turning Point* (1977) generated *seven* acting nominations in a single year, the most ever for a director.

FIFTY TOTAL ACTING NOMINATIONS AND WINS

1. William Wyler

- 36 nominations (1936-1968)
- 14 wins

THIRTY-THREE TOTAL ACTING NOMINATIONS AND WINS

2. Elia Kazan

- 24 nominations (1945-1961)
- 9 wins

TWENTY-NINE TOTAL ACTING NOMINATIONS AND WINS

3. Martin Scorsese

- 24 nominations (1974-2019)
- 5 wins

TWENTY-SIX TOTAL ACTING NOMINATIONS AND WINS

4. George Cukor

- 21 nominations (1930-1972)
- 5 wins

5. Fred Zinnemann

- 20 nominations (1944-1977)
- 6 wins

TWENTY-FIVE TOTAL ACTING NOMINATIONS AND WINS

6. Woody Allen

- 18 nominations (1977-2013)
- 7 wins

TWENTY-TWO TOTAL ACTING NOMINATIONS AND WINS

7. Sidney Lumet

- 18 nominations (1962-1988)
- 4 wins

TWENTY TOTAL ACTING NOMINATIONS AND WINS

8. George Stevens

- 18 nominations (1935-1959)
- 2 wins

9. Mike Nichols

- 18 nominations (1966-2007)
- 2 wins

10. Billy Wilder

- 17 nominations (1944-1966)
- 3 wins

10 Greatest Directors of All Time

In the section for Best Pictures we presented a list that used four criteria to create a list called "8 Greatest Movies of All Time." Now we add up the data summarized in the previous five lists—Best Director nominations, Best Director wins, Best Picture nominations, Best Picture wins, acting nominations, and acting wins—to identify the ten greatest directors ever.

The two Best Picture criteria are based on the notion that the director is more responsible than anyone else for creating a Best Picture nominee and winner. Other Oscar categories add to or subtract from an Oscar-caliber movie, but they don't shoulder the same load the director does. Just to name one example, Katharine Hepburn won more Best Actress Oscars than anybody and is second in Best Actress nominations, but in sixty-two years of making movies she never appeared in a single Best Picture winner. The best acting, just like the best cinematography and the best makeup and the best music, does not necessarily make a Best Picture.

Applying the six criteria—Best Director nominations and wins, Best Picture nominations and wins, acting nominations and wins—yields ten G.D.O.A.T. In the following list, we don't attempt to "weight" the criteria—say, two points for an Oscar win, just one for a nomination—but even if we did, William Wyler would still be way ahead of runner-up Martin Scorsese. Just on the outside and looking in is the trio of Frank Capra, Clint Eastwood, and David Lean, who all tallied thirty-one.

81 TOTAL

1. William Wyler

- 12 Best Director nominations + 3 Best Director wins + 13 Best Picture nominations + 3 Best Picture wins + 36 acting nominations + 14 acting wins

49 TOTAL

2. Martin Scorsese

- 9 BD noms + 1 BD win + 9 BP noms + 1 BP win + 24 acting noms + 5 acting wins

48 TOTAL

3. Elia Kazan

- 5 BD noms + 2 BD wins + 4 BP noms + 4 BP wins + 24 acting noms + 9 acting wins

45 TOTAL

4. Steven Spielberg

- 9 BD noms + 2 BD wins + 13 BP noms + 1 BP win + 17 acting noms + 3 acting wins

43 TOTAL

5. Fred Zinnemann

- 7 BD noms + 2 BD wins + 6 BP noms + 2 BP wins + 20 acting noms + 6 wins

40 TOTAL

6. George Cukor

- 5 BD noms + 1 BD win + 7 BP noms + 1 BP win + 21 acting noms + 5 acting wins

37 TOTAL

7. Woody Allen

- 7 BD noms + 1 BD win + 3 BP noms + 1 BP win +18 acting noms + 7 acting wins

8. Billy Wilder

- 8 BD noms + 2 BD wins + 5 BP noms + 2 BP wins + 17 acting noms + 3 wins

36 TOTAL

9. John Ford

- 5 BD noms + 4 BD wins + 9 BP noms + 1 BP win + 12 acting noms + 5 acting wins

34 TOTAL

10. George Stevens

- 6 BD noms + 2 BD win + 6 BP noms + 0 BP win + 18 acting noms + 2 acting wins

6 Directors Who Won the Best Director Oscar with Their First Movie

Like young outsiders dramatically vaulting over the wall and into the center of the Oscar arena, the following directors won the Academy Award for Best Director with their *first* feature films ("young," because everyone on the list was under forty-five at the time, in fact half of them were under thirty-six).

Another twenty-two prominent directors, including Warren Beatty, Kenneth Branagh, Sidney Lumet, Mike Nichols, and one woman, Emerald Fennell—*Promising Young Woman* (2020)—almost made the list, but they were nominees, not winners, for their directorial debuts. Jerome Robbins at number six is unique because *West Side Story* was not only the first movie he directed, it was the *only* movie he directed.

1. James L. Brooks, *Terms of Endearment* (1983)
2. Kevin Costner, *Dances with Wolves* (1990)
3. Delbert Mann, *Marty* (1955)
4. Sam Mendes, *American Beauty* (1999)
5. Robert Redford, *Ordinary People* (1980)
6. Jerome Robbins, *West Side Story* (1961)

Ordinary People (1980).

3 Average Ages of Best Director Winners

Typically very young directors aren't put in charge of expensive high-profile movies that garner Oscars. Best Director winners in the 1920s and '30s were mostly in their mid-thirties, and then for the next six decades they were mostly in their forties. In the first two decades of the twenty-first century directors averaged more than fifty years old, so the trend is definitely going older.

This next list shows the average ages for all ninety-eight Best Director winners in the years of the ceremonies that presented them with their awards. If that number ninety-eight seems odd, considering there have been only ninety-five Academy Awards ceremonies, three of the ceremonies—the first (held in 1929), the thirty-fourth (held in 1962), and the eightieth (held in 2008)—had double winners. All the individual directors listed below were the exact age being discussed, or they were the closest director to that age, with their ages in parentheses. See the list called "12 Average Ages of Winners in the Acting Categories" on page 237 for a similar list.

1. Winner's average age

Forty-seven years old
- Robert Benton (47), *Kramer vs. Kramer* (1979)

- John Ford (47), *The Grapes of Wrath* (1940)
- Steven Spielberg (47), *Schindler's List* (1993)
- George Stevens (47), *A Place in the Sun* (1951)
- Robert Wise (47), *West Side Story* (1961)

2. Winner's average age for early three-decade period

1930s (the first complete decade of winners) to 1950s: forty-three years old

- John Huston (42), *The Treasure of the Sierra Madre* (1948)
- Frank Lloyd (44), *The Divine Lady* (1928)

3. Winner's average age for recent three-decade period

1990s-2010s: fifty years old

- Ethan Coen (50), *No Country for Old Men* (2007)

4 Directors Nominated for Best Director Twice *in the Same Year*

It's rare when a director is nominated twice in the same year, but it's happened four times. Only once since the 1930s, though, which makes Steven Soderbergh's double nomination extra special. Note that one of these chronologically listed directors was actually nominated *three* times in the same year. The movies that brought a win for Best Director are marked **Winner**.

1. Frank Lloyd

Second ceremony (held in 1930)
- **Winner** *The Divine Lady* (1928)
- *Drag* (1929)
- *Weary River* (1929)

2. Clarence Brown

Third ceremony (held in 1930)
- *Anna Christie* (1930)
- *Romance* (1930)

3. Michael Curtiz

Eleventh ceremony (held in 1939)
- *Angels with Dirty Faces* (1938)
- *Four Daughters* (1938)

4. Steven Soderbergh

Seventy-third ceremony (held in 2001)
- **Winner** *Traffic* (2000)
- *Erin Brockovich* (2000)

10 Directors Who Directed Two Best Picture-Nominated Movies *in the Same Year*

Spread out through all ninety-five years of the Academy Awards are ceremonies where one director directed two of the movies up for that year's Best Picture honor. As shown below, one of these directors, Sam Wood, achieved that feat *twice*. And look at that 1941 ceremony (starting at number five), with three directors responsible for *six* Best Picture nominees, including the winner.

Note also how different some pairs of movies are: the two at number four, for instance, are so unlike each other they could be from two different directors. The greatest directors, like the greatest artists in other artistic fields, can't be confined.

1. Ernst Lubitsch

Fifth ceremony (held in 1932)
- *One Hour with You* (1932)
- *The Smiling Lieutenant* (1931)

2. Jack Conway

Ninth ceremony (held in 1937)
- *Libeled Lady* (1936)
- *A Tale of Two Cities* (1935)

3. Michael Curtiz

Eleventh ceremony (held in 1939)
- *The Adventures of Robin Hood* (1938)
- *Four Daughters* (1938)

4. Victor Fleming

Twelfth ceremony (held in 1940)
- **Winner** *Gone with the Wind* (1939)
- *The Wizard of Oz* (1939)

5. John Ford

Thirteenth ceremony (held in 1941)
- *The Grapes of Wrath* (1940)
- *The Long Voyage Home* (1940)

6. Alfred Hitchcock

Thirteenth ceremony (held in 1941)
- **Winner** *Rebecca* (1940)
- *Foreign Correspondent* (1940)

7. Sam Wood

Thirteenth ceremony (held in 1941)
- *Kitty Foyle* (1940)
- *Our Town* (1940)

Fifteenth ceremony (held in 1943)
- *Kings Row* (1942)
- *The Pride of the Yankees* (1942)

8. Francis Ford Coppola

Forty-seventh ceremony (held in 1975)
- **Winner** *The Godfather: Part II* (1974)
- *The Conversation* (1974)

9. Herbert Ross

Fiftieth ceremony (held in 1978)
- *The Goodbye Girl* (1977)
- *The Turning Point* (1977)

10. Steven Soderbergh

Seventy-third ceremony (held in 2001)
- **Winner** *Traffic* (2000)
- *Erin Brockovich* (2000)

8 Directors Who Won the Best Director Oscar for Directing a Musical

Here's a test to see how good a musical is—watch the musical numbers with the sound turned off. If the director has done his job, then you won't even need to hear the song for the scene to be imaginative and memorable. Success like this is harder to achieve than you think, because fewer than 10 percent of the Best Director winners won that Oscar for directing a musical.

Listed below are those Best Directors and their winning musicals, listed chronologically to show how the musical genre has really changed.

And changed it has. Consider that in the decade of movies from 1958 to 1968, half of the Best Director wins were for musicals, whereas since 1973 there has only been *one* winner for a musical.

That long forty-four-year gap between numbers seven and eight roughly parallels the general slump in movie musicals that set in around the early 1980s and lasted until *Chicago* (2002) won for Best Picture two decades later. High-profile non-nominated flops like *Xanadu* (1980) and *Grease 2* (1982) didn't kill off the genre, but they certainly wounded it for a while.

1. Leo McCarey, *Going My Way* (1944)
2. Vicente Minnelli, *Gigi* (1958)
3. Jerome Robbins and Robert Wise, *West Side Story* (1961)
4. George Cukor, *My Fair Lady* (1964)
5. Robert Wise, *The Sound of Music* (1965)

6. Carol Reed, *Oliver!* (1968)

7. Bob Fosse, *Cabaret* (1972)

8. Damien Chazelle, *La La Land* (2016)

5 Times Co-Directors of One Movie Were Nominated for Best Director

Co-directors have been credited on many popular movies. Among them are these three Oscar-winning movies: William Dieterle and Max Reinhardt's *A Midsummer Night's Dream* (1935); Jonathan Dayton and Valerie Faris's *Little Miss Sunshine* (2006); and Richard Glatzer and Wash Westmoreland's *Still Alice* (2014). Best Picture nominees *How the West Was Won* (1962) and *The Longest Day* (1962) were actually credited to *three* directors each.

What's special about these next directing duos is that in each case two people got Best Director nominations for the same movie; the two Best Director-winning pairs are noted.

1. Thirty-fourth ceremony (held in 1962)

- **Winners** Jerome Robbins and Robert Wise, *West Side Story* (1961)

2. Fifty-first ceremony (held in 1979)

- Warren Beatty and Buck Henry, *Heaven Can Wait* (1978)

3. Eightieth ceremony (held in 2008)

- **Winners** Ethan Coen and Joel Coen, *No Country for Old Men* (2007)

4. Eighty-third ceremony (held in 2011)

- Ethan Coen and Joel Coen, *True Grit* (2010)

5. Ninety-fifth ceremony (held in 2023)

- **Winners** Dan Kwan and Daniel Scheinert, *Everything Everywhere All at Once* (2022)

9 Directors Nominated for Directing and Acting Oscars in the Same Year

Nobody has won directing *and* acting Oscars in the same year, but all the names on this list did get nominations in both categories simultaneously. Warren Beatty and Clint Eastwood even accomplished this double-nomination feat *twice*.

In the following list for directing and acting, nominated categories and movies follow the names, and the **Winner** symbol immediately precedes a winning category. Note that two of the Best Director nominees below, Roberto Benigni and Laurence Olivier, directed themselves to Best Actor wins. Also observe that George Clooney was nominated in both categories at the same ceremony, but they were for different movies.

1. Woody Allen

- **Winner** Best Director and Best Actor: *Annie Hall* (1977)

2. Warren Beatty

- Best Director and Best Actor: *Heaven Can Wait* (1978)
- **Winner** Best Director and Best Actor: *Reds* (1981)

3. Roberto Benigni

- Best Director and **Winner** Best Actor: *Life Is Beautiful* (1997)

4. Kenneth Branagh

- Best Director and Best Actor: *Henry V* (1989)

5. George Clooney

- Best Director: *Good Night, and Good Luck.* (2005)
- **Winner** Best Supporting Actor: *Syriana* (2005)

6. Kevin Costner

- **Winner** Best Director and Best Actor: *Dances with Wolves* (1990)

7. Clint Eastwood

- **Winner** Best Director and Best Actor: *Unforgiven* (1992)

Unforgiven (1992).

- **Winner** Best Director and Best Actor: *Million Dollar Baby* (2004)

8. Laurence Olivier

- Best Director and **Winner** Best Actor: *Hamlet* (1948)

9. Orson Welles

- Best Director and Best Actor: *Citizen Kane* (1941)

6 Directors Who Directed Their Spouses to Best Actress Nominations

These six alphabetically listed husbands directed their wives to Oscar nominations for Best Actress.

We haven't included husbands with their nominated girlfriends or live-in relationships, which is why Jules Dassin and Melina Mercouri, whose marriage was still six years away when he directed her to a Best Actress nomination in *Never on Sunday* (1960), aren't on the list. Also missing are Tim Robbins and Susan Sarandon, who were together but weren't married when he directed her to a Best Actress Oscar in *Dead Man Walking* (1995).

As you'll see from the list of directors, nominated spouses, and nominated movies, only once did one of those nominations lead to a win. Interestingly, there's no similar list of wives who directed their husbands to Oscar nominations for Best Actor, because that's never happened.

1. Richard Brooks

- Jean Simmons, *The Happy Ending* (1969)

2. John Cassavetes

- Gena Rowlands, *A Woman Under the Influence* (1974)
- Gena Rowlands, *Gloria* (1980)

3. Joel Coen

- **Winner** Frances McDormand, *Fargo* (1996)

4. Paul Czinner

- Elisabeth Bergner, *Escape Me Never* (1935)

5. Blake Edwards

- Julie Andrews, *Victor Victoria* (1982)

6. Paul Newman

- Joanne Woodward, *Rachel, Rachel* (1968)

12 Breakthroughs for the Best Director Oscar

Some of the other lists in this section about directors lament the conspicuous omissions; this next list celebrates directors whose Oscar appearance represented some kind of breakthrough. Maybe the lament here is how long it took to achieve some of these breakthroughs, or how much time passed between the first nomination for a pioneer and the eventual first win.

1. First director of a "talkie" to win for Best Director

Lewis Milestone
- *All Quiet on the Western Front* (1930)
- Several movies with sound and spoken dialogue had been nominated for Best Director at the second ceremony (held early in 1930), but at the third ceremony (held late in 1930) *All Quiet on the Western Front* became the first all-talking movie to win for Best Director.

2. First woman nominated for Best Director

Lina Wertmüller
- *Seven Beauties* (1975)
- Women—including prominent names like Dorothy Arzner, Ida Lupino, and Elaine May—were directing successful movies as far back as the silent era, but the wary Academy welcomed them with folded arms, so not one woman was nominated in this category before Wertmüller.
- Later women nominated for Best Director: Jane Campion, Sofia Coppola, Kathryn Bigelow, Greta Gerwig, Emerald Fennell, and Chloé Zhao.
- The ninety-third ceremony (held in 2021) was the first ceremony to have two women (Fennell and Zhao) nominated for Best Director.

3. First woman to win for Best Director

Kathryn Bigelow
- *The Hurt Locker* (2008)
- Chloé Zhao—*Nomadland* (2020)—and Jane Campion—*CODA* (2021)—are the only other women to win the Best Director Oscar (and they won in back-to-back years).

4. First woman to direct a movie that won for Best Picture

Kathryn Bigelow
- *The Hurt Locker* (2008)
- Chloé Zhao is the only other woman to have directed a Best Picture-winning movie.
- Randa Haines was the first woman to direct a Best Picture nominee: *Children of a Lesser God* (1986).

5. First Black director nominated for Best Director

John Singleton
- *Boyz n the Hood* (1991)
- No Black director has ever won in this category.

6. First Black director to direct a movie that won for Best Picture

Steve McQueen
- *12 Years a Slave* (2013)

7. First person to win two Oscars for Best Director

Frank Borzage
- *7th Heaven* (1927)
- *Bad Girl* (1931)

8. First person to win consecutive Oscars for Best Director

John Ford
- *The Grapes of Wrath* (1940)
- *How Green Was My Valley* (1941)
- Later directors to win consecutive Oscars: Joseph L. Mankiewicz and Alejandro G. Iñárritu.

9. First director of a foreign-language film nominated for Best Director

Federico Fellini
- *La Dolce Vita* (1960), in Italian
- Bong Joon-ho is the first director of a foreign-language film that won for Best Director: *Parasite* (2019), in Korean.

10. First ceremony when every Best Director nominee was born in a foreign country

Sixtieth ceremony (held in 1988)
- Bernardo Bertolucci (born in Italy), *The Last Emperor* (1987)
- John Boorman (England), *Hope and Glory* (1987)
- Lasse Hallström (Sweden), *My Life as a Dog* (1985)
- Norman Jewison (Canada), *Moonstruck* (1987)
- Adrian Lyne (England), *Fatal Attraction* (1987)

11. Youngest and oldest Best Director winners

Damien Chazelle (32)
- *La La Land* (2016)
- John Singleton (24) is the youngest nominee: *Boyz n the Hood* (1991).

Clint Eastwood (74)
- *Million Dollar Baby* (2004)
- John Huston (79) was the oldest nominee: *Prizzi's Honor* (1985).

BEST WRITING

17 Major Developments in the Best Writing Category

A separate book could be written about the Oscars presented for screenwriting. Of all the original categories at the Academy Awards, this is the one that has changed the most. The screenwriting category started as three separate awards, was then consolidated into one award, later split into two and then three separate categories, recombined again, and endured many name changes. Here's how this category has evolved over the decades, plus the first winners after each change was made (when there are two or more Oscar-winning co-writers, they're presented alphabetically).

1. First ceremony (held in 1929)

The Academy launched its Oscar ceremonies with three writing categories, but the one for Best Title Writing (honoring the interstitial text cards shown in silent movies) would end after this first year as "talkies" quickly supplanted silent movies.

- Best Title Writing: Joseph Farnham (no specific movie)
- For adapted screenplays, Best Writing (Adaptation): Benjamin Glazer, *7th Heaven* (1927)
- For original screenplays, Best Writing (Original Story): Ben Hecht, *Underworld* (1927)

2. Second ceremony (held in 1930)

Immediately the Academy made its first changes to the initial writing categories. For the second and third ceremonies, the Academy presented just a single Oscar for writing.

- Best Writing: Hans Kraly, *The Patriot* (1928)

3. Fourth ceremony (held in 1931)

Picking up on a distinction made at the first ceremony, the Academy split the single writing award into two categories to acknowledge the difference between a screenplay adapted from a previous source and an original screenplay.

- For adapted screenplays, Best Writing (Adaptation): Howard Estabrook, *Cimarron* (1931)
- For original screenplays, Best Writing (Original Story): John Monk Saunders, *The Dawn Patrol* (1930)

4. Eighth ceremony (held in 1936)

For the eighth ceremony, the Academy changed the name of the award for adaptations to Best Writing (Screenplay).

- For adapted screenplays, Best Writing (Screenplay): Dudley Nichols, *The Informer* (1935)
- For original screenplays, Best Writing (Original Story): Ben Hecht and Charles MacArthur, *The Scoundrel* (1935)

5. Thirteenth ceremony (held in 1941)

Next, the Academy created a third writing category, Best Writing (Original Screenplay), and changed Best Writing (Original Story) so that it recognized the source material for adapted screenplays, which were already being honored with the Oscar for Best Writing (Screenplay). Consequently, it was possible for a movie with an adapted screenplay to win two Oscars, one for the original material and one for the adaptation. This happened at the fourteenth ceremony (held in 1942) when *Here Comes Mr. Jordan* (1941) won two Best Writing Oscars, one for the playwright Harry Segall to honor his original play *Heaven Can Wait*, and another for the screenwriters Sidney Buchman and Seton I. Miller for adapting Segall's play. Here are the first winners of the three categories at the thirteenth ceremony.

- For adapted screenplays, Best Writing (Original Story): Benjamin Glazer and John S. Toldy, *Arise, My Love* (1940)
- For adapted screenplays, Best Writing (Screenplay): Donald Ogden Stewart, *The Philadelphia Story* (1940)
- For original screenplays, Best Writing (Original Screenplay): Preston Sturges, *The Great McGinty* (1940)

6. Fifteenth ceremony (held in 1943)

A slight adjustment to the category honoring the original material used for adapted screenplays: Best Writing (Original Story) became Best Writing (Original Motion Picture Story). One of the nominees in this newly named writing category was Irving Berlin, who was nominated for his original story idea for *Holiday Inn* (1942); Berlin's "White Christmas" from the same movie won that year's Best Music (Song) Oscar.

- For adapted screenplays, Best Writing (Original Motion Picture Story): Emeric Pressburger, *49th Parallel*, aka *The Invaders* (1941)
- For adapted screenplays, Best Writing (Screenplay): George Froeschel, James Hilton, Claudine West and Arthur Wimperis, *Mrs. Miniver* (1942)
- For original screenplays, Best Writing (Original Screenplay): Michael Kanin and Ring Lardner Jr., *Woman of the Year* (1942)

7. Twenty-first ceremony (held in 1949)

The Academy condensed the Best Writing categories from three to two. Out was Best Writing (Original Screenplay). In (with a name change) were Best Writing (Motion Picture Story) for original screenplays and Best Writing (Screenplay) for adaptations. These two categories lasted all of one year.

- For adapted screenplays, Best Writing (Screenplay): John Huston, *The Treasure of the Sierra Madre* (1948)
- For original screenplays, Best Writing (Motion Picture Story): Douglas Morrow, *The Search* (1948)

8. Twenty-second ceremony (held in 1950)

A year after it reduced the writing categories to two, the Academy immediately expanded them back to three, one for adapted screenplays, one for the source materials for adapted screenplays, and one for original screenplays.

- For adapted screenplays, Best Writing (Motion Picture Story): Richard Schweizer and David Wechsler, *The Stratton Story* (1949)
- For adapted screenplays, Best Writing (Screenplay): Joseph L. Mankiewicz, *A Letter to Three Wives* (1949)
- For original screenplays, Best Writing (Story and Screenplay): Robert Pirosh, *Battleground* (1949)

9. Twenty-ninth ceremony (held in 1957)

The Academy clarified two of the three categories by changing their names and adding helpful dashes. Best Writing (Screenplay) became Best Writing (Screenplay—Adapted), and Best Writing (Story and Screenplay) became Best Writing (Screenplay—Original).

- For adapted screenplays, Best Writing (Motion Picture Story): Dalton Trumbo, *The Brave One* (1956)

- For adapted screenplays, Best Writing (Screenplay—Adapted): John Farrow, S.J. Perelman and James Poe, *Around the World in 80 Days* (1956)
- For original screenplays, Best Writing (Screenplay—Original): Albert Lamorisse, *The Red Balloon* (1956)

10. Thirtieth ceremony (held in 1958)

Again the Academy reduced three writing categories to two, this time adding cumbersome new names that again used dashes.

- For adapted screenplays, Best Writing (Screenplay—Based on Material from Another Medium): Pierre Boulle, Carl Foreman and Michael Wilson, *The Bridge on the River Kwai* (1957)
- For original screenplays, Best Writing (Story and Screenplay—Written Directly for the Screen): George Wells, *Designing Woman* (1957)

11. Forty-second ceremony (held in 1970)

Another awkward name change, this time using eight words to say, basically, "original."

- Best Writing (Screenplay—Based on Material from Another Medium): Waldo Salt, *Midnight Cowboy* (1969)
- Best Writing (Story and Screenplay—Based on Material Not Previously Published or Produced): William Goldman, *Butch Cassidy and the Sundance Kid* (1969)

12. Forty-third ceremony (held in 1971)

Pity the poor presenter at the forty-third ceremony who read out the new name for the "original screenplay" category, which the Academy had expanded to a *sixteen*-word title.

- Best Writing (Screenplay—Based on Material from Another Medium): Ring Lardner Jr., *M*A*S*H* (1970)

- Best Writing (Story and Screenplay—Based on Factual Material or Material Not Previously Published or Produced): Francis Ford Coppola and Edmund H. North, *Patton* (1970)

13. Forty-seventh ceremony (held in 1975)

Somebody probably figured out that the televised Oscar ceremony, which many viewers complained was too long, could be shortened considerably by reducing the Best Writing (Story and Screenplay—Based on Factual Material or Material Not Previously Published or Produced) category to simply Best Writing (Original Screenplay). *Voilà*, sixteen words to four. The adapted screenplay category was similarly shortened from nine words to seven.

- Best Writing (Screenplay Adapted from Other Material): Francis Ford Coppola and Mario Puzo, *the Godfather: Part II* (1974)
- Best Writing (Original Screenplay): Robert Towne, *Chinatown* (1974)

14. Forty-ninth ceremony (held in 1977)

The two sleek new writing categories got tweaked again, including the addition of the longest title yet for original screenplays.

- Best Writing (Screenplay—Based on Material from Another Medium): William Goldman, *All the President's Men* (1976)
- Best Writing (Screenplay Written Directly for the Screen—Based on Factual Material or on Story Material Not Previously Published or Produced): Paddy Chayefsky, *Network* (1976)

15. Fifty-first ceremony (held in 1979)

The Academy streamlined the twenty-one word title, tweaked the other one, and took the dashes out of both. These changes would last for thirteen years.

- Best Writing (Screenplay Based on Material from Another Medium): Oliver Stone, *Midnight Express* (1978)
- Best Writing (Screenplay Written Directly for the Screen): Nancy Dowd, Robert C. Jones and Waldo Salt, *Coming Home* (1978)

16. Sixty-fourth ceremony (held in 1992)

The Academy's only revision was to the name of the category honoring adapted screenplays.

- Best Writing (Screenplay Based on Material Previously Produced or Published): Ted Tally, *The Silence of the Lambs* (1991)
- Best Writing (Screenplay Written Directly for the Screen): Callie Khouri, *Thelma & Louise* (1991)

***The Silence of the Lambs* (1991).**

17. Seventy-fifth ceremony (held in 2003)

After constantly shifting the writing categories for three-quarters of a century, the Academy finally settled on the simplest and clearest names. These are the two writing categories still honored today.

- Best Writing (Adapted Screenplay): Ronald Harwood, *The Pianist* (2002)
- Best Writing (Original Screenplay): Pedro Almodóvar, *Talk to Her* (2002)

7 Best Picture-Winning Movies That Weren't Nominated for Best Writing

At eighty-eight of the ninety-five Academy Awards ceremonies, the myriad Best Writing categories have included a writing nomination for the movie that eventually won for Best Picture. That leaves seven ceremonies when the Best Writing categories somehow excluded the Best Picture winner. The seven Best Picture winners that weren't even nominated for a writing award are listed below in chronological order along with the movie that actually won (the specific writing category is shown with that year's name).

1. *Wings* (1927)
- Best Writing (Original Story): *Underworld* (1927)
2. *The Broadway Melody* (1929)
- Best Writing: *The Patriot* (1928)
3. *Grand Hotel* (1932)
- Best Writing (Adaptation): *Bad Girl* (1931)
4. *Cavalcade* (1933)
- Best Writing (Adaptation): *Little Women* (1933)
5. *Hamlet* (1948)
- Best Writing (Screenplay): *The Treasure of the Sierra Madre* (1948)

6. ***The Sound of Music* (1965)**
- Best Writing (Screenplay—Based on Material from Another Medium): *Doctor Zhivago* (1965)

7. ***Titanic* (1997)**
- Best Writing (Screenplay Written Directly for the Screen): *Good Will Hunting* (1997)

17 Movies That Were Nominated for a Single Oscar— Best Writing—and Won

The generic category Best Writing has actually been represented at the Academy Awards by many different names and subdivisions. Six of those variations, everything from Best Writing (Motion Picture Story) to Best Writing (Original Screenplay) are represented in the following chronological list of movies that won a Best Writing Oscar without being nominated in any other category. The most recent of these movies came out in 1957, which makes some sense; at the thirtieth Oscar ceremony (held in 1958), the Academy reduced the number of Best Writing categories from three to two, thus eliminating one of the categories that might bring a movie a single nomination.

1. *Underworld* (1927)
2. *The Dawn Patrol* (1930)
3. *One Way Passage* (1932)
4. *Manhattan Melodrama* (1934)
5. *The Scoundrel* (1935)
6. *The Great McGinty* (1940)
7. *Princess O'Rourke* (1943)
8. *Marie-Louise* (1944)
9. *The House on 92nd Street* (1945)
10. *The Seventh Veil* (1945)
11. *Vacation from Marriage* (1945)

12. *The Bachelor and the Bobby-Soxer* (1947)

13. *The Stratton Story* (1949)

14. *Panic in the Streets* (1950)

15. *Seven Days to Noon* (1950)

16. *The Red Balloon* (1956)

17. *Designing Woman* (1957)

4 Streaks of Screenwriting Nominations for Three or More Consecutive Years

In the long history of the Oscars, only three screenwriters have been nominated for a Best Writing Oscar for at least three consecutive years. To compile this list we treated the Best Writing (Adapted Screenplay) and Best Writing (Original Screenplay) categories as one generic screenwriting award. Winners are noted.

Paul Haggis is shown below with movies that look like they competed in the same year, but they didn't. While *Million Dollar Baby* and *Crash* are both listed as 2004 movies, *Crash* came out too late in the year for the mandatory one-week screening in Los Angeles that the Academy requires for eligibility, so it was bumped into competition with movies that really were released in 2005.

FOUR YEARS IN A ROW

1. Woody Allen

- *Broadway Danny Rose* (1984)
- *The Purple Rose of Cairo* (1985)
- **Winner** *Hannah and Her Sisters* (1986)
- *Radio Days* (1987)

THREE YEARS IN A ROW

2. Woody Allen

- **Winner** *Annie Hall* (1977)
- *Interiors* (1978)
- *Manhattan* (1979)

3. Robert Towne

- *The Last Detail* (1973)
- **Winner** *Chinatown* (1974)
- *Shampoo* (1975)

4. Paul Haggis

- *Million Dollar Baby* (2004)
- **Winner** *Crash* (2004)
- *Letters from Iwo Jima* (2006)

The King's Speechwriters: 2 Screenwriters with Double-Digit Nominations for Best Writing

The following list is just for Best Writing nominations, with wins listed below each winner's name. Both of the screenwriters listed below got additional nominations and wins in other categories: *Annie Hall* (1977) brought Woody Allen a Best Actor nomination and a Best Director win in addition to his screenwriting Oscar, and Billy Wilder had eight Best Director nominations overall, but those non-writing nominations aren't counted here. We've combined all variations of the Best Writing category—including the different adapted screenplay, original screenplay, and story subcategories—into a single total.

Screenwriting superstars who came close to making the list include John Huston, the Coen brothers, Francis Ford Coppola, Oliver Stone, and Robert Towne, who wrote what's often called the greatest screenplay of all time, the serpentine *Chinatown* (1974). Heading up the list of screenwriters with the most nominations without ever winning a Best Writing Oscar is Federico Fellini with eight.

SIXTEEN NOMINATIONS

1. Woody Allen

- *Annie Hall* (1977)
- *Hannah and Her Sisters* (1986)
- *Midnight in Paris* (2011)

TWELVE NOMINATIONS

2. Billy Wilder

- *The Lost Weekend* (1945)

- *Sunset Boulevard* (1950)
- *The Apartment* (1960)

The Apartment (1960).

20 Prominent Authors Who Were Nominated for Best Writing

Hollywood has often recruited established writers of novels and short stories to write screenplays. The results have been inconsistent. Ray Bradbury, Truman Capote, Roald Dahl, Joan Didion, William Faulkner, F. Scott Fitzgerald, Joseph Heller, Aldous Huxley, Stephen King, Ayn Rand, J.K. Rowling, Nathanael West, Thornton Wilder, and other titans of twentieth century fiction all wrote movie screenplays without getting any Oscar nominations for their work.

However, the following twenty writers of prominent novels and/or short stories *did* get nominated in one of the various Best Writing categories, with their nominated movies (including the seven Oscar winners) noted. In a few cases the nominations were shared with other people—James Hilton, author of the best-selling novel *Lost Horizon*, was one of four Oscar-winning co-writers of *Mrs. Miniver* (1942), for example.

1. James Agee

- *The African Queen* (1951)

2. Raymond Chandler

- *Double Indemnity* (1944)
- *The Blue Dahlia* (1946)

3. Arthur C. Clarke

- *2001: A Space Odyssey* (1968)

4. Richard Condon

- *Prizzi's Honor* (1985)

5. Pat Conroy

- *The Prince of Tides* (1991)

6. Fannie Flagg

- *Fried Green Tomatoes* (1991)

7. Graham Greene

- *The Fallen Idol* (1948)

8. Dashiell Hammett

- *Watch on the Rhine* (1943)

Double Indemnity (1944).

9. James Hilton

- **Winner** *Mrs. Miniver* (1942)

10. Nick Hornby

- *An Education* (2009)
- *Brooklyn* (2015)

11. John Irving

- **Winner** *The Cider House Rules* (1999)

12. Larry McMurtry

- *The Last Picture Show* (1971)
- **Winner** *Brokeback Mountain* (2005)

13. Vladimir Nabokov

- *Lolita* (1962)

14. Dorothy Parker

- *A Star Is Born* (1937)
- *Smash-Up: The Story of a Woman* (1947)

15. S.J. Perelman

- **Winner** *Around the World in 80 Days* (1956)

16. Mario Puzo

- **Winner** *The Godfather* (1972)
- **Winner** *The Godfather: Part II* (1974)

17. Jean-Paul Sartre

- *The Proud and the Beautiful* (1953)

18. Sidney Sheldon

- **Winner** *The Bachelor and the Bobby-Soxer* (1947)

19. John Steinbeck

- *Lifeboat* (1944)
- *A Medal for Benny* (1945)
- *Viva Zapata!* (1952)

20. Donald E. Westlake

- *The Grifters* (1990)

20 Prominent Playwrights Who Were Nominated for Best Writing

Everyone on this list wrote (or co-wrote) an Oscar-nominated screenplay; in addition, all twenty playwrights won a Pulitzer Prize for Drama and/or a competitive Tony Award, Broadway's highest honor. Nominated movies (including the fourteen Oscar winners) are noted.

Some notable playwrights who also wrote Oscar-nominated (and even Oscar-winning) screenplays—famous names like Woody Allen, Paddy Chayefsky, Noël Coward, Lillian Hellman, Garson Kanin, Terence Rattigan, and George Bernard Shaw—aren't included because they didn't win a Pulitzer or a competitive Tony for their stage work. Note Neil Simon at number sixteen, four nominations but no wins. Neil Simon never won a Best Writing Oscar, seriously? Also think of who's missing from the list, only the most famous playwright of all time. That's right, William Shakespeare has never been nominated for an Oscar despite his many movie credits, including one as the sole writer of Laurence Olivier's Best Picture-winning *Hamlet* (1948).

1. George Abbott

- *All Quiet on the Western Front* (1930)

2. Robert Bolt

- **Winner** *Doctor Zhivago* (1965)
- **Winner** *A Man for All Seasons* (1966)

3. Horton Foote

- **Winner** *To Kill a Mockingbird* (1962)
- **Winner** *Tender Mercies* (1983)
- *The Trip to Bountiful* (1985)

4. William Gibson

- *The Miracle Worker* (1962)

5. Christopher Hampton

- **Winner** *Dangerous Liaisons* (1988)
- *Atonement* (2007)

- **Winner** *The Father* (2020)

6. Moss Hart

- *Gentleman's Agreement* (1947)

7. William Inge

- **Winner** *Splendor in the Grass* (1961)

The Father (2020).

8. Tony Kushner

- *Munich* (2005)
- *Lincoln* (2012)
- *The Fabelmans* (2022)

9. Alan Jay Lerner

- **Winner** *Gigi* (1958)
- *My Fair Lady* (1964)

10. David Mamet

- *The Verdict* (1982)
- *Wag the Dog* (1997)

11. Arthur Miller

- *The Crucible* (1996)

12. John Osborne

- **Winner** *Tom Jones* (1963)

13. William Saroyan

- **Winner** *The Human Comedy* (1943)

14. Peter Shaffer

- *Equus* (1977)
- **Winner** *Amadeus* (1984)

15. John Patrick Shanley

- **Winner** *Moonstruck* (1987)
- *Doubt* (2008)

16. Neil Simon

- *The Odd Couple* (1968)
- *The Sunshine Boys* (1975)
- *The Goodbye Girl* (1977)
- *California Suite* (1978)

17. Tom Stoppard

- *Brazil* (1985)
- **Winner** *Shakespeare in Love* (1998)

18. Alfred Uhry

- **Winner** *Driving Miss Daisy* (1989)

19. Tennessee Williams

- *A Streetcar Named Desire* (1951)
- *Baby Doll* (1956)

20. August Wilson

- *Fences* (2016)

20 Actors and Actresses Nominated for Best Writing

The prominent actors and actresses listed below were also Oscar nominees in one of the Best Writing categories. A few major screenwriters who also acted—familiar names such as John Cassavetes, John Huston, Buck Henry, Spike Lee, Elaine May, and Orson Welles—aren't included here because they were predominantly writers or directors who also had some interesting movie roles, but acting was not their main claim to fame. John Huston, for example, had eight Best Screenplay nominations (with one win) and five Best Director nominations (again with one win) while also playing some memorable supporting roles in *The Cardinal* (1963) and *Chinatown* (1974), among others. Since he would have to be considered a writer/director first and an actor second, he's not on the list.

Of the actors and actresses who are listed below with their Oscar-nominated/Oscar-winning screenplays, three of them—George Clooney, Ruth Gordon, and Alec Guinness—won acting Oscars but didn't win for screenwriting. Only Emma Thompson at number sixteen has won both an acting Oscar—Best Actress for *Howards End* (1992)—and a screenwriting Oscar.

1. Ben Affleck and Matt Damon

- **Winner** *Good Will Hunting* (1997)

2. Sacha Baron Cohen

- *Borat* (2006)
- *Borat Subsequent Moviefilm* (2020)

3. Warren Beatty

- *Heaven Can Wait* (1978)
- *Reds* (1981)
- *Bulworth* (1998)

4. Kenneth Branagh

- *Hamlet* (1996)
- *Belfast* (2021)

5. Charles Chaplin

- *The Great Dictator* (1940)
- *Monsieur Verdoux* (1947)

6. George Clooney

- *Good Night, and Good Luck.* (2005)
- *The Ides of March* (2011)

7. John Cleese

- *A Fish Called Wanda* (1988)

8. Bradley Cooper

- *A Star Is Born* (2018)

9. Julie Delpy and Ethan Hawke

- *Before Sunset* (2004)
- *Before Midnight* (2013)

10. Peter Fonda and Dennis Hopper

- *Easy Rider* (1969)

11. Ruth Gordon

- *A Double Life* (1947)
- *Adam's Rib* (1949)
- *Pat and Mike* (1952)

12. Alec Guinness

- *The Horse's Mouth* (1958)

13. Maggie Gyllenhaal

- *The Lost Daughter* (2021)

14. Sarah Polley

- *Away from Her* (2006)
- **Winner** *Women Talking* (2022)

15. Sylvester Stallone

- *Rocky* (1976)

16. Emma Thompson

- **Winner** *Sense and Sensibility* (1995)

17. Billy Bob Thornton

- **Winner** *Sling Blade* (1996)

18. Kristen Wiig

- *Bridesmaids* (2011)

19. Gene Wilder

- *Young Frankenstein* (1974)

20. Owen Wilson

- *The Royal Tenenbaums* (2001)

6 Foreign-Language Movies That Won Oscars for Best Writing

The Oscar for Best Writing (in all of its variations, including adapted screenplays and original screenplays) hasn't always gone to an English-language movie. Eighty-eight times a movie made primarily in a foreign language has gotten a screenplay nomination, and, as shown below, six of those nominees have won.

The list of eighty-eight Best Writing nominees is Euro-centric, with over half of the movies coming from Austria, France, Germany, Spain, Sweden, and Switzerland. France has the most nominations, twenty-eight, followed closely by Italy's twenty-four. Familiar titles among the eighty-one include these from different countries: France's *Children of Paradise* (1945); Algeria's *Z* (1969); Sweden's *Cries and Whispers* (1972); West Germany's *Das Boot* (1981); Italy's *Life Is Beautiful* (1997); Brazil's *City of God* (2002); and Mexico's *Roma* (2018). Those were nominees; here are the winners, in chronological order.

1. Switzerland's *Marie-Louise* (1944)
2. France's *The Red Balloon* (1956)
3. Italy's *Divorce Italian Style* (1961)
4. France's *A Man and a Woman* (1966)
5. Spain's *Talk to Her* (2002)
6. South Korea's *Parasite* (2019)

7 Movies That Changed My Life, Selected by Oscar-Winner Bruce Joel Rubin

Often screenwriters seem to pick a lane and stay in it. They write teen horror films, or screwball comedies, or dignified dramas, etc. With *Ghost* (1990), Bruce Joel Rubin successfully jumped lanes and genres with a smart supernatural thriller that also presented one of the screen's classic romances while simultaneously accomplishing two things that are often mutually exclusive—it won Oscars (including one for his screenplay) and became the year's highest-grossing movie. While Bruce's paragraphs below touch on his fascinating personal story, he writes in more detail about his adventurous life, his other movies, and his journey to becoming a meditation teacher and photographer at his website, brucejoelrubin.com. We contacted him to ask about the movies that had influenced him, which he discusses here and then lists.

"My first movie was *The Jolson Story* when I was four years old. I demanded that my parents stay in the theater with me and watch it twice. I was smitten. One day I learned that my grandmother's first cousin was married to Al Warner, one of the Warner Bros. I would watch the credits for Warner Bros. cartoons at Saturday matinees and yell out, to no one in particular, that they were my cousins. I felt destined for Hollywood.

"But as I grew older, I sensed that movies were mostly fun and diversionary. I had yet to see *Casablanca* or *The African Queen*, among a host of films I later came to love. The only directors whose names I knew were Hitchcock and DeMille. And then in the tenth grade I tagged along with some influential friends to an art house in Detroit and saw Ingmar Bergman's *Wild Strawberries*, and the world of cinema opened up before me. I took a film class my first year of college and saw *Citizen Kane* and *La Strada* and began to sense that this was the world I needed to enter. I transferred to NYU alongside classmates Marty Scorsese and Brian de Palma. That is when we all discovered Truffaut's *Jules and Jim*, Fellini's *8 ½*, and Lean's *Lawrence of Arabia*.

"After that I was addicted to film as an essential art form. It's also when I began to understand the greatness of Hollywood. Marty Scorsese and I would talk for hours. He knew every costume designer, cinematographer, and film editor on every movie ever made. I realized how little I knew and, more problematically, how little I, as a future filmmaker, had to say. Then I took an unexpected massive dose of LSD and returned from what I sensed was a death and rebirth experience with my eyes looking on a totally different landscape. I asked why I had come back from the dead and a deep inner voice told me it was so that I could tell people what I saw. In that strange otherworldly experience, I had begun to find my voice.

"But equally important, Hollywood had found a new voice as well. It had evolved from the home of 'movies' into the world of 'cinema' and I wanted more than anything to be part of it. The list of films that awakened me to this new storytelling power is far too long to present here, but I list some of them below in the order that I saw them. I remain endlessly grateful to them all."

1. *Wild Strawberries* (1957)
2. *Citizen Kane* (1941)
3. *Casablanca* (1942)
4. *L'Avventura* (1960)
5. *Jules and Jim* (1962)
6. *Lawrence of Arabia* (1962)
7. *The Godfather* (1972)

16 Breakthroughs for the Best Writing Oscar

A celebration of Oscar nominations and wins that represented some kind of breakthrough in the Best Writing category. All the iterations of this Oscar—its various adaptation and original subcategories—have been subsumed under a general Best Writing heading.

1. First "talkie" to win for Best Writing

The Big House (1930)

- One year prior to Frances Marion's win, Hans Kraly won the Best Writing Oscar for *The Patriot* (1928), a mostly silent film with some limited dialogue. *The Big House*, however, is considered the first true "talkie" to win in a writing category.

2. First comedy to win a Best Writing Oscar

It Happened One Night (1934)

- The most recent comedy to win a Best Writing Oscar: *Jojo Rabbit* (2019).

3. First musical to win a Best Writing Oscar

An American in Paris (1951)

- No other musical has won a Best Writing Oscar, although several others have been nominated, most recently *La La Land* (2016).

4. First animated movie nominated for a Best Writing Oscar

Toy Story (1995)

- No animated movie has ever won a Best Writing Oscar, although several other animated movies have been nominated, most recently *Inside Out* (2015).

5. First movie in a foreign language to win a Best Writing Oscar

France's *The Red Balloon* (1956)
- Most recent movie in a foreign language to win a Best Writing Oscar: South Korea's *Parasite* (2019).

6. First movie and sequel to both win Best Writing Oscars

The Godfather (1972)
- *The Godfather: Part II* (1974)

7. First woman to win a Best Writing Oscar

Frances Marion
- *The Big House* (1930)
- Marion's Oscar two years later—*The Champ* (1931)—made her the first person to win two Best Writing Oscars.

8. First person with a solo screenwriting credit on a Best Picture winner

Howard Estabrook
- *Cimarron* (1931)
- Siân Heder is the only woman who was listed as the sole screenwriter on a Best Picture-winning movie: *CODA* (2021).

9. First Black screenwriter to win for Best Writing

Geoffrey Fletcher
- *Precious* (2009)
- Lonne Elder III and Suzanne de Passe were the first Black screenwriters with Best Writing nominations: *Sounder* (1972) and *Lady Sings the Blues* (1972), respectively.

10. First writing team to win a Best Writing Oscar

Victor Heerman and Sarah Y. Mason

- *Little Women* (1933)
- As of the ceremony held in 2023, there have been 205 Best Writing Oscars handed out in the various writing categories (Adapted Screenplay, Original Screenplay, Motion Picture Story, etc.). About two-thirds went to solo screenwriters, and the rest went to writing partners or writing "teams" (whose members may or may not have been working together).

11. First four-member writing team to win Best Writing Oscars for one movie

Ian Dalrymple, Cecil Lewis, W. P. Lipscomb, and George Bernard Shaw, *Pygmalion* (1938)

- The most recent movie with a four-member writing team to win Best Writing Oscars: *BlacKkKlansman* (2018).
- A four-member team is the largest to win Best Writing Oscars. The largest writing team all nominated together is the nine-member team nominated for Best Writing (Adapted Screenplay): *Borat Subsequent Moviefilm* (2020).

12. First person nominated in three Best Writing categories in the same year

Emeric Pressburger

- Best Writing (Original Motion Picture Story): *49th Parallel,* aka *The Invaders* (1941)
- Best Writing (Original Screenplay): *One of Our Aircraft Is Missing* (1942)
- Best Writing (Screenplay): *49th Parallel,* aka *The Invaders* (1941)

- At the fifteenth Academy Awards ceremony (held in 1943), Pressburger won in the first category listed above. No other screenwriter has ever duplicated Pressburger's triple-nomination feat.

13. First people to win two Best Writing Oscars at the same ceremony

Pierre Collings and Sheridan Gibney
- Best Writing (Original Story) and Best Writing (Screenplay): *The Story of Louis Pasteur* (1936)
- These two categories were intended to represent the original source material and its adaptation; Collings and Gibney are the only two screenwriters to win both categories in the same year.

14. First person to win consecutive Oscars for Best Writing

Joseph L. Mankiewicz
- *A Letter to Three Wives* (1949)
- *All About Eve* (1950)
- Robert Bolt later duplicated Mankiewicz's feat with two adapted screenplays: *Doctor Zhivago* (1965) and *A Man for All Seasons* (1966).

15. First person to write two consecutive Best Picture winners

Paul Haggis
- Seventy-seventh ceremony (held in 2005): *Million Dollar Baby* (2004)
- Seventy-eighth ceremony (held in 2006): *Crash* (2004)

16. Youngest and oldest Best Writing winners

Ben Affleck (25)

- *Good Will Hunting* (1997)

James Ivory (89)

- *Call Me by Your Name* (2017)
- Ivory is the oldest winner ever in any Oscar category.
- Ivory is the oldest Oscar winner, but the oldest nominee in any category is John Williams, who was 90 when his Best Music (Original Score) nomination for *The Fabelmans* (2022) was announced in early 2023.

START OF INTERMISSION . . .